D1519158

TIMBERRR...

TIMBERRR...

A History of Logging in New England

Mary Morton Cowan

The Millbrook Press
Brookfield, Connecticut

To Erin, Patrick, Matthew, and Kaitlyn, who are learning to love Great-Grandpa's woods

Library of Congress Cataloging-in-Publication Data
Cowan, Mary Morton.
Timberrr...a history of logging in New England / by Mary Morton
Cowan.
p. cm.
Summary: An illustrated history of the New England forests, from colo-
nial days when settlers freely used the trees for warmth and housing to
today's tensions between environmentalists and the logging industry.
Includes bibliographical references (p.   ).
ISBN 0-7613-1866-6 (lib. bdg.)
1. Logging—New England—History—Juvenile literature. [1. Logging—
New England—History. 2. Forests and forestry—New England—History.
3. New England—History.] I. Title.
SD538.2.N35 C68 2003
634.9'8'0974—dc21   2002014540

Published by The Millbrook Press, Inc.
2 Old New Milford Road
Brookfield, Connecticut 06804
www.millbrookpress.com

Printed in the United States of America
5 4 3 2 1

CONTENTS

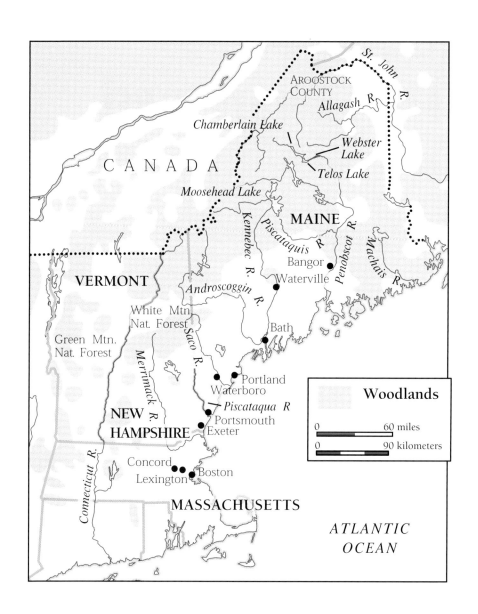

St. John R.

AROOSTOCK
COUNTY

Allagash R.

Chamberlain Lake

Webster
Lake

Telos Lake

CANADA

Moosehead Lake

MAINE

Kennebec R.

Piscataquis R.

Penobscot R.

Machais R.

Bangor

Waterville

VERMONT

Androscoggin R.

White Mtn.
Nat. Forest

Bath

Green Mtn.
Nat. Forest

Saco R.

Merrimack R.

Portland
Waterboro

Piscataqua R

NEW
HAMPSHIRE

Portsmouth
Exeter

Concord

Boston

Connecticut R.

Lexington

MASSACHUSETTS

ATLANTIC
OCEAN

Woodlands

0   60 miles

0   90 kilometers

Chapter 1

TREES EVERYWHERE!

The earth rumbles. Trucks loaded high with logs roar along northern New England roads. Logging is big business today, not without its controversy. There is a wide range of opinion as to how, or *if*, trees should be harvested. America's logging industry began almost as soon as the first Europeans settled here. It was controversial then, too.

When explorers first spied the northern North American coast, they were impressed by its limitless trees. A thousand years ago, Vikings cut trees on the Canadian coast to build settlements in Greenland. In the early 1600s, Samuel de Champlain wrote that islands off the New England coast were covered with a variety of trees. On the Maine coast, Henry Hudson cut a tree to replace a mast on his first voyage to the New World in 1609.

The forest stretched for thousands of miles. Trees were everywhere. They grew right to the water's edge. Here and there, a clearing could be found—a salt marsh or a sandy plain. Particularly in southern New England, large American Indian clearings could be seen at the mouths of wide rivers, although some cornfields were spotted as far north as Penobscot Bay. The rest was trees.

To European settlers, the forest was frightening. They had lived in light, open areas, with meadows and gardens. Here the forest

As beautiful as the forest appears to us on a sunny winter day, it was a barrier to early European immigrants.

was dark and spooky underneath towering trees. In places it was hard to walk, the forest floor was so snarled with vines and prickly underbrush. Settlers had to continuously clear their way, what with fallen debris and tree stumps. In winter, trudging through deep snow was exhausting. To make things worse, it was easy to get lost in the woods.

Settlers felt monsters lurking everywhere. At night, frogs, toads, and crickets were so loud, people could not sleep. Trees made eerie creaks and groans. Winds whistled and howled during storms. Tree trunks snapped loudly in the bitter cold of winter. In summer, lightning struck with a vengeance, ripping huge pine trees into shreds. Frightening wild animals roamed about—wolves, wildcats, bears, and foxes. They devoured the settlers' sheep and chickens. Strange people peeked out from behind trees and bushes—and occasionally those people terrified the newcomers by attacking their homesteads or by stealing their provisions. To top it off, settlers were tormented by poison ivy and biting insects.

These new immigrants could hardly stand the forest. They agreed with William Bradford, who came on the *Mayflower,* that this was a "hideous and desolate wilderness." Yet they had to do something to survive—for in northern New England, the forest was all there was.

As hideous as the forest seemed, settlers found some trees had edible nuts or sweet sap. With help from American Indians, they learned how to survive in the forest. There was good hunting and fishing—and if the forest could be tamed, it would provide shelter and warmth. Settlers did what they had to do. They took to logging. Axes in hand, they chopped down trees.

First they cleared enough land to grow a few crops. They used the logs to make homes for their families and shelters for their animals. The forest, once an enemy, became their means of survival. Hefty oxen hauled logs out of the woods, uprooted stumps, and dragged boulders aside to make way for cornfields. Slowly, arduously, settlers changed the landscape.

The earliest New Englanders settled at the edge of the sea, or along the shores of easily accessible rivers, such as the Piscataqua

Early New Englanders relied on wooden sailing ships for trade and travel.

and the Merrimack. They cut timber and masts to build ships. From the start, lumbering and shipbuilding were integrated, and thus they remained for almost three hundred years. By 1676, Boston had thirty master shipwrights and wooden ships were still being built in Maine more than 240 years later—as late as World War I. Bath, Maine, on the Kennebec River, already a shipbuilding community in pre-Revolutionary War times, is still a major site for building navy destroyers.

More and more settlers moved to New England, amounting to about 20,000 in the 1630s. Later arrivals had to settle farther inland, along the Merrimack, the Connecticut, and other rivers.

Northern New England is ill-suited for farming. Only plant species that are adapted to cool, short growing seasons and winter temperatures as low as -40°F (-40°C) can survive. Retreating glaciers from the last ice age created thousands of rivers and lakes. They also left a motley assortment of rocks and ledges, sand and gravel—and very thin soil. Trees thrive, but little else. It was natural, then, that wherever people settled, lumbering followed.

When the Pilgrims' ship, *Fortune,* sailed back to England after the first winter, it was loaded with pine clapboards. By 1631 logging began along the Saco and Piscataqua rivers. Sawmills were built in every new settlement, and colonists quickly discovered a market for lumber. They exported planks, boards, barrel staves, and other wood products to England, where there was a severe wood shortage. They traded lumber in the West Indies for molasses, sugar, and rum. Colonists made a good profit burning wood to make potash and selling it to England for its glass and textile industries. Lots more trees were cut and burned to make charcoal for blast furnaces needed to smelt iron, and for fuel for blacksmiths to make tools.

New England colonists found a wide variety of evergreens and deciduous trees. It was, however, the white pine, *pinus strobus,* that drew their attention. You cannot miss pine trees. They dominate the landscape wherever they grow. Even today, they grow taller than other trees, and they often grow in clumps, called stands. Settlers found an abundance of them along the New Hampshire and southern Maine coast, from the Merrimack River to the Kennebec. To the colonists, those pine trees were monstrous, much larger than any trees they had ever seen. Many seemed to reach almost to the sky—over 150 feet (46 meters). That is as high as a ten-story building. They were 3 to 5 feet (1 to 1.5 meters) thick, and they had no branches for 50 to 60 feet (15 to 18 meters) above the ground. Some were more than three hundred years old.

Cutting and moving those pines was a mammoth undertaking. The trees were too large to easily fell, or cut down, and getting them out of the woods was a treacherous task. Settlers who learned to harvest that timber became America's first lumbermen and river drivers.

A Day in the Life of...

A COLONIAL BOY

"Mornin', Jude," you say as you enter the hovel. "Mornin', Justin." Both young steers lift their heads to greet you. You squirm your fingers into their rusty-red hair to feel their soft warmth. After you fill their hayracks and water buckets, they grunt and start chewing. Your two old oxen, Bright and Broad, are not here. Father has already yoked them up and driven to town with a wagonload of lumber to sell.

Every day you work your steers—except Sundays, of course. Jude and Justin were born last year in this very hovel, just after your ninth birthday. When you started training the calves, they wore the small yoke Father made to train Bright and Broad four years ago. Now your steers have grown so big, they need a larger yoke. You must train them well, for Father cannot work without oxen. He will have to butcher his team next year or the following one. Oxen are incredibly strong, but Father says they usually go lame before they are seven. Bright and Broad are already five.

Father started clearing this land as soon as he arrived in Massachusetts Bay. That was in 1630, the year before you were born. Chopping down all those trees and building a cabin and hovel has taken years. With a growing family, Father needs still more land cleared for crops. Mother is frightened of the woods, and she doesn't like you in them, but she knows you must help Father. Your younger brothers will one day help, too. Soon your five-year-old brother will learn to clear underbrush, as you did. He already stacks firewood beside the cabin.

It's time to yoke up. Jude steps forward and leans into the yoke. It takes a little coaxing to step Justin in, but finally you get the yoke onto their necks and the bows snapped in place. The chain jingles when you connect it to the ring. Some men drive their oxen hard, whacking them often with the goad. Father can just speak to Bright and Broad, and they will obey. You are training Jude and Justin that way, too. Only rarely must you whip them.

"Hi-yeee," you shout, raising them. "Hi-yeee." You guide your young team toward the trees you and Father felled yesterday, always keeping to their left, as

12

you were taught. There are tree stumps and boulders to move. "Back, Jude. Back, Justin." Slowly they back up to a huge stump. You and Father dug around it yesterday and cut some of the roots. Now you attach the chain to it, then raise your oxen again. Into that yoke they bend, heads down, straining in quick, short grunts. They lean so far forward, their chests almost scrape the ground. But they cannot pull out the stump. You hack at another tree root with your ax, but still the stump will not budge. Jude loses his balance and jerks to his knees. "Whoa," you cry quickly, so Justin won't twist his neck in the yoke. Your neighbor's team had to be put down last year after one stumbled and strangled the other in the yoke.

There are smaller stumps to pull, and before long Jude and Justin have ripped several out of the earth. For hours you work that field, hauling stumps and boulders to the edge. Toward noon, you take off your sweaty wool jacket, but the mosquitoes are so fierce, you quickly cover up again. Jude and Justin browse while you sit on the stone wall to eat the lunch Mother packed. Tomorrow, Bright and Broad will have to remove the huge stump. Then you and Father will chop down more trees and the oxen will haul them to the saw pit. You will help Father saw boards for days, until he has another wagonload to sell. As usual, you will stand in the pit and pull the two-man saw down, then Father will pull it up. Down and up you will go a million times, until your shoulders ache and you are covered with sweat and sawdust.

Back at the hovel, you unyoke your team, curry and feed them. You check their hooves to be sure no pebbles or splinters have caught in the clefts, or that their shoes have come loose. "Good night, Jude. Good night, Justin."

On your way to the cabin, you smell wood smoke. Your mother and sisters will have venison stew and corn cakes cooking on the fire. When Father sees all you did today, he will be proud—and so will you.

Chapter 2

THE KING'S WOODS

Forests in the British Isles had been depleted long before English settlers came to America. Britain imported what timber it needed. That included lumber for ships and masts for her Royal Navy. A single warship required three masts 100 or more feet (30 meters) tall, plus three topmasts on top of those, a huge bowsprit, and yardarms for all the topsails.

Suitable mast trees grew in the nearby eastern Baltic countries. But, in times of war, the entrance to the Baltic Sea was blocked to British ships. New England's white pines were amazingly tall. Shorter Baltic timber had to be pieced together to make masts. New England pines were more costly to transport than Baltic masts, but the American colonies were a reliable source, for they belonged to Britain.

Early on, colonists traded lumber freely with England and other countries. New England's first cargo of masts was shipped to England in 1634. Before many years, a mast trade developed.

The Royal Navy contracted for masts and spars with British merchants, who appointed mast agents in the colonies. Agents, in turn, made deals with colonists to hire actual cutting and hauling crews.

Getting suitable masts was not easy. A finished mast had to be 1 yard (1 meter) tall for every inch in diameter. Once a tree was chopped down, mast loggers measured its length and cut the limbs and top off before hauling it out.

At the mast landing, mastwrights shaped the huge logs into sixteen-sided masts, using special axes and adzes. Spars with diameters less than 20 inches (51 centimeters) were hewn into eight sides. Finally, hundreds of tons of masts and spars were loaded onto enormous ships, built especially to carry masts. They sailed in convoys to England and other British colonies. All this work provided jobs for colonists, but the big profits went to the mast agents and to the merchants in England.

England grew ever more desperate for masts. When William and Mary came to the throne in 1689, they stepped up naval construction. To control the colonies' mast pines, they initiated what became known as the Broad Arrow Policy. It was part of the Second Charter of Massachusetts Bay, which included the District of Maine, and was enacted in 1691. All white pine trees 24 inches (61 centimeters) or more in diameter, measuring 12 inches (30 centimeters) from the ground, on lands not already granted to "private persons," were reserved for the Royal Navy.

A surveyor general was sent to the colonies to mark every eligible tree with the king's ancient symbol, the Broad Arrow. That meant boating along every major river—the Merrimack, the Piscataqua, the Saco, and more—to chop three slashes into the bark of every 24-inch (61-centimeter) pine tree within a few miles of the rivers, or to etch an arrow with a hot branding iron. The task was impossible. This was no hundred-acre wood. There were millions of acres of forest and thousands of miles of navigable

The King's Broad Arrow

Surveyors hacked the king's Broad Arrow symbol into large white pines. The man at the left is measuring a tree's circumference. Pines larger around than 6.25 feet (1.9 meters) were marked.

rivers and coastline. No one man with a few deputies could hope to control such an area.

In addition, the surveyor was to impose a £100 fine for every tree cut without permission. In colonial times, money was extremely scarce, so most people traded goods for other goods. A farmer or unskilled laborer might earn only £10 cash in a year. At that rate, it would take ten years for one man to earn enough to pay such a fine.

For the next thirty-eight years, England tightened restrictions to the policy. More colonies were included and more severe punishments were added. In the end, England forbade cutting pines of *any* size, not on private land.

For many years the primary shipping port was Portsmouth, New Hampshire, at the mouth of the Piscataqua River. By 1700, masting crews had to trek 20 miles (32 kilometers) or more from the river to get a good mast, so surveyors followed the pine eastward to the Saco and Presumpscot rivers and beyond. By 1727 Falmouth (now Portland, Maine) became an important masting center and led the mast trade by 1772.

Over the decades, one surveyor general followed another. Surveyor John Bridger, with four deputies, did manage to mark over three thousand mast pines with the royal Broad Arrow insignia, but few were actually shipped. Once, at Exeter, New Hampshire, he found that of seventy pines his men had marked, all but one had been illegally cut and hauled away. Not a single settler knew anything about it. "All the people on the frontier depend on the woods for their livelihood," he wrote to King

George I. "They say the King has no woods here, hence they will cut what and where they please."

Colonists were outraged by every one of the royal restrictions. They had struggled to tame this forest. They remembered arriving in New England with woefully inadequate tools. By the early 1700s colonial blacksmiths had forged new, heavier axheads, weighing up to 7 pounds (3 kilograms). Long, curved hickory handles fit a woodchopper's grasp. Colonists had become skilled at felling trees, and they had made lumbering a profitable livelihood. Pines brought more money as cut up lumber than as masts. No one from England or anywhere else was going to tell them they could not cut those trees!

Colonists came up with a number of ways to evade the law. They burned stands of huge pines, just enough to singe them and make them unsuitable for the king's masts but usable for lumber. They formed townships, with absentee landlords, to create more "private" land, thus reducing the king's woods. The Crown claimed townships were not private. Colonists insisted they were.

Knowing surveyors could not be everywhere at once, colonists cut the mast pines anyway. Surveyors could seldom prove who stole the timber. Once a tree was cut, floated downriver and put through a sawmill, no one could tell where it came from. To further hide evidence, colonists sawed boards just under 24 inches (61 centimeters), so surveyors could not prove they came from a large tree.

David Dunbar was likely the most hated surveyor of all. In 1730 he arrived in Maine with armed forces. He burned people's homes and raided sawmills in order to seize timber. Colonists despised

Mast loggers chopped down smaller trees to soften the fall of a huge mast pine. Then two men felled it, or chopped it down.

Mast roads came through towns on the way to mast depots at the ocean shore. Oxen had to swing wide so that long masts could make the turn. Some New England villages still have triangular "town squares," shaped long ago by oxen hauling masts.

him. Once, after his deputies seized some illegally cut timber at Exeter, New Hampshire, a band of colonists disguised themselves as natives, entered the pub where the officers were drinking, and attacked them. Outside, other men cut the rigging of Dunbar's boat, and gouged a hole in the bottom. Dunbar and his men barely made it back to Portsmouth before their boat sank.

Colonists were not the only stumbling blocks in getting mast pines to England. The trees themselves posed problems. Many large, old pines are rotten inside, full of ants. Before blazing one with the Broad Arrow mark, a surveyor tapped it with the blunt end of his ax. If it sounded hollow, he knew the tree was worthless. Often, however, it was impossible to tell whether a pine was suitable until after it had been cut down. Most were defective.

Felling, or bringing down, a giant mast tree was tough. Many split when they landed, despite bedding the fall with smaller trees. Hauling a mast out of the woods was a grueling process, using twelve to forty yoke of oxen. A lot of oxen were strangled in the process. Going down rivers caused still more damage. A huge log could easily be gouged by boulders in the riverbed or cracked or splintered going over rapids. Even if the mast got all the way to tidewater, cutting it to shape might damage it enough to render it unfit for the Royal Navy.

If a mast pine was defective, parts of it might be usable for smaller spars, bowsprits, or yardarms, or perhaps sawed into boards. Often it was simply left in the woods to rot. Sometimes, even when a log was sound, it was too big to be hauled or floated out of the woods. A lot of white pine was wasted.

Large ships were built to transport masts. Up to fifty hewn masts, plus smaller spars, were loaded through a large hole in the stern of each ship. After ships were loaded, men closed and sealed the holes.

When shots rang out at Lexington and Concord, that settled it. The Revolutionary War was on! No more masts for England! On an island in Boston Harbor, colonists burned the spars that were awaiting shipment to England. At mast depots along the coast they hid masts by towing them upriver to shallow water. Patriots in Falmouth refused to let Britain have masts or outfit any more British ships. Britain retaliated by bombarding the town, leaving it in ashes. But the king got no masts. Masts were still rotting in Portland Harbor fifty years later.

All things considered, the Broad Arrow Policy was one of the earliest, and continuous, causes of rebellion against Great Britain. To New Englanders, it was a primary cause of the Revolutionary War.

A MAST LOGGER

Your nostrils tingle in the frosty air as you lead your oxen, Dan and Pete, into the woods.

As you trudge along, you remember what Clem, the mast boss, told Mama yesterday. "I hear your boy's good with them oxen," he said. "They're the best span around these parts. I'll be needin' him to help get a big one out o' the woods. We've built a hovel and a camp up the road a few miles. We'll have that monster down to Stroudwater Landing by next week. Don't fret none." He promised you'd earn two shillings a day, plus more for your oxen.

You know Mama will fret. Neighbor Jackson went masting last summer and never did come back. Got crunched under the stick, they said. But she agreed to let you go, for the family needs money. "You're the man now, since Pa died," she says.

Swampers have cut down brush, hauled rocks off to the side, and filled some gullies to make as level and straight a road as they can to move the monstrous pine out. At the site you notice evergreens lying where the tree will fall. "Bedding crew cut that yesterday," explains Silas, another mast logger. "Nice and soft, so she won't crack when she falls."

Two choppers are going at it, in perfect rhythm— *CHOP-back, CHOP-back.* Chips fly through the air. Soon the men scramble off to the side, yelling "TIMBERRR!" Slowly, the mighty pine tilts, then falls with a thunderous roar. It springs up once from its bed of boughs, then drops with a final thud, dead. "Yaa-hoooo!" everyone roars, jumping around and swearing a blue streak. "By cracky," roars Clem, "she's sound! The last nine or ten sticks were hollow t' the core."

"Takes some doin' to get one o' these monsters out without breaking 'er all to smithereens," says Silas.

You watch while a couple of men measure the length of the enormous log. Then they chop the top off and trim the rest of the limbs.

"Load 'er up," Clem shouts. "Shove them wedges in. Harder!" Crews inch the monstrous mast up onto four sleds.

"Hook on up front," Clem says, so you lead Dan and Pete to the head of the line. Clem always has the strongest team lead, so he can swing them around to the tail going down slopes. "Yoke up!" Clem bellows to the crew. Thirty oxmen thwack their goads at once. Silas spits lots of tobacco juice and yells himself blue in the face. "Get in there, you lazy lummox." Clem keeps hollering until all thirty yokes of oxen are up. "Hi-yeeee! Line up them beasts!" Dan and Pete, and all the other teams, lean into their yokes.

The mast rumbles as it moves forward. Ox chains jingle, their sound echoing through the cold, snowy woods.

Going uphill, some men strike their animals hard with goads to force them on. No wonder Pa called them bullwhackers. "Whoa!" screams Clem as you near the crest of the hill. You shift your oxen to the rear, as told, to help keep the load on track going down. Clem wraps a snub line around a big tree to hold the massive log back, so it won't get out of control and wreck everything. The teams up front get hung up in the air before the front end of the mast tips down over the brow of the hill. Finally, you make it.

Before long, Clem's yelling again. "Dag nab it! A chain broke!" He's raving mad. A team is down, twisted in its yoke. One ox cannot get up. "Leg's broken," Clem mutters. He clunks the downed ox between its eyes with the blunt end of his ax. You wince. Clem looks at you and says, "He's a goner." A new yoke of oxen, waiting alongside, steps right in and on you go. You worry about Dan and Pete.

You heave a sigh of relief when Clem bellows, "Unyoke." It's time to gather kindling and boil tea. First you tend to Dan and Pete. You polish their horns, just as Pa did every day. They chomp away on hay while you eat your vittles.

There are more miles to trek before you reach the mast landing. Now, in the makeshift hovel, you snuggle between Dan and Pete, exhausted. Their rhythmic breathing lulls you to sleep.

Chapter 3

TIMBERRR!

Oh, the lumberman's life is a wearisome one,
Though some call it free from care.
'Tis wielding the axe from morning till night,
In the middle of the forest so drear;
It is lying in the camp so bleak and cold,
While the wintry winds do blow,
And as soon as the morning star doth appear,
To the wild woods we must go.

"Lumberman's Song" sung across America and eastern Canada [This version comes from Rangeley, Maine, c. 1903]

After the Revolutionary War, Massachusetts granted war veterans extensive acreage in the District of Maine. Settlers moved up the rugged Androscoggin and Kennebec river valleys and others. Loggers took to the woods at a great rate, to make a profit from the forest resources. Thanks to the mast trade, the skills of cutting and moving logs were developed well before 1700. Woodsmen still cut some masts, some for export, some for our new country's ships—*Old Ironsides*, and others.

At first, farmers and their sons logged, using their own draft animals. Early logging camps had three or four men and a few yoke of oxen. Soon, camps included a boss, choppers, swampers, and teamsters. Later, cooks, cookees (cooks' helpers), scalers, and others were added. They were a diverse bunch—Yankees, Penobscot Indians, Canadians (New Brunswickers, Acadians, PEIs [Prince Edward Islanders], and Québécois), and other immigrants. In 1850 there were more than 8,600 men and 6,700 animals logging in the Maine woods. Logging was going on in New Hampshire and Vermont as well. Camps were rough, work was dangerous, living conditions deplorable, and men were paid very low wages.

Woods near most major rivers in New England were heavily logged in the nineteenth century, from the Connecticut to the

Machias in eastern Maine. Most of the state of Connecticut was cleared. Woodsmen cut logs for lumber to build homes and businesses for our growing country. Three quarters of the houses in the northern United States were built of pine, and 75 percent of that came from Maine's Penobscot watershed.

Everyone sold lumber by the board foot. A board foot is the amount of wood in one square foot of a 1-inch (2.5-centimeter)-thick board. In 1835, Maine lumbermen cut almost 82 million board feet of lumber, averaging 354 board feet per log. That's more than 231,000 big logs!

Demand for wood took its toll on the New England forests. With American industrialization and urban expansion, more wood was needed for building. Millions of trees were cut for fuel until coal was widely used in the mid-1800s. Lumbermen kept chopping.

For much of the mid-nineteenth century, the northern forest produced more timber than anywhere else in the world. It was Maine's Penobscot River that set the records. The Penobscot drainage basin covers 10,000 square miles (25,400 square kilometers), almost one third of the state of Maine. Massive log drives were driven down the Penobscot and its tributaries. Some years, the cut totaled over 200 million board feet. Along the river near Bangor, sawmills sliced up all the logs, and ships loaded with lumber sailed for ports near and far. Between 1832 and 1888, a total of 8.7 billion board feet of lumber was shipped from Bangor. Bangor was the most bustling, roaring lumber town in the world!

Logging camps, like the one shown above, operated from November to March. Women sometimes accompanied their husbands to camp and worked as cooks and laundresses for the loggers.

Early in the twentieth century, there were upwards of one hundred men in a camp. Most operations added a saw filer to the crew and a blacksmith to shoe horses, repair bunk chains, whiffletrees, and other iron equipment. By 1920 large logging operations had up to 150 men and 100 animals.

When a company wanted to set up a logging operation, a cruiser was sent out to survey the land. Off he went, compass and ax in hand, and a knapsack slung over his back. His job was to estimate the amount of timber, determine where hauling roads could be built, and find a spot for the camp. He paced off acres and counted trees. He figured where landings could go, and how much work needed to be done to a stream to get logs downriver. For weeks at a time, the cruiser hiked through the woods surveying woodlands, fording streams, and climbing through underbrush. All the while, he had to watch for bears and wolves.

Logging camps were built in late summer when, hopefully, those wretched little insects known as no-see-ums were gone. During bug season, men covered themselves with layers of tar mixed with grease to keep from being eaten alive. Swamping crews removed stumps and rocks to build tote roads. Twitching roads were carefully planned. They were narrow trails for a single horse to twitch (drag) a log from the tree stump to a yard.

The yard had to be cleared, giving plenty of turnaround space so horses would not have to back up. Steep trails wound back and forth. Wide hauling roads were made for double sleds to haul logs from yards to landings. On low spots of ground, swampers built corduroy roads. They placed long hemlock logs, called stringers,

Swampers built corduroy roads. The long stringers were hemlock. Shorter cross pieces were cut from maple or birch, or other nearby trees.

over the mud hole, then put short logs crosswise, close together on top of the stringers. Sleds traveled over them easily once they were covered with snow.

Crews cleared debris away from banks and out of streams, so they could get logs downriver. Sometimes rocks had to be blasted out, and occasionally they actually changed where the water flowed. Hay was cut for the animals, and camps were ready to operate before the first snowfall.

The toughest logger in any camp was the boss. He was responsible for the logging operation. Men called him the "Bull of the Woods." He bellowed orders, often in rough language and manner. But a fair boss was respected, rough or not. There was high morale in his camp, and his crews sweated long and hard to stack the landings with logs!

Whenever there were several camps in one operation, a walking boss, or superintendent, had charge of them all. Before telephone lines were installed between camps, he had to ride horseback for miles to reach all his crews.

Every logging crew had one or two swampers to keep logging roads in good shape. Hauling roads had to be frozen solid for horses to haul loaded sleds. New trails needed to be cut as logging progressed. Turnoff areas had to be kept shoveled, so teams could pass one another. On slopes, teamsters often wrapped chains around their sled runners to add friction. They called them bridle chains. Swampers had to follow close behind with shovels to fill in the ruts.

Scalers were important to the financial success of any logging operation. It was the scaler who calculated how much timber was cut, and lumbermen's pay depended on his calculations. Scaling was measuring, not weighing, as the name may suggest. Logs were scaled several times—at the yard, again at the landing, once more downriver at the sorting booms, and finally again on delivery at the sawmill. The first tool for measuring logs by the board foot came in the early 1800s. Several rules developed, whose measurements varied slightly. Some rules were long measuring sticks, with rows of numbers to calculate the board footage that could be sawed from a log. One rule was a long handle with a ten-spoked wheel on the end. The scaler ran the wheel along the log to measure its length. He then measured the log's diameter and calculated the board footage, using the scale on the handle. This rule became popular in Maine and elsewhere, sometimes with different names.

Most often it was the scaler who marked all the logs at the landing with his company's initials or identifying symbol. With his ax, he chopped through the bark near both ends of each log. Unusually long logs were marked in the middle, too. A company's symbol might be an *X*, a diamond, a cross, or two parallel lines—anything that could be made with an ax. When the logs arrived at the sorting booms at the end of the river drive, everyone could tell whose logs were whose, and the right company would be paid.

It took years of experience to become a skillful scaler. Once long logs gave way to 4-foot (1.2-meter)-long pulpwood, the scaler's job changed. Stamping hammers were made to brand logs on the ends, and measurements shifted from board footage to cords.

As important as all the logging jobs were, cutting crews were at the heart of it all. A cutting crew consisted of choppers, a teamster, and a swamper. The head chopper made the undercut into the tree in the direction he wanted the tree to fall. Other choppers cut from the back side, then limbed it (trimmed off branches) so the log could be twitched without snagging. They bucked the fallen tree (cut it into logs), for horses to twitch away, one at a time.

Early logging crews included hewers, a remnant of masting days. The hewer trimmed the tree into a square length of timber, using a heavy broadax. It wasted so much wood, the practice was stopped in the mid-nineteenth century.

The Bangor Rule was one of the early rules used to measure the amount of lumber in a log. The top row of numbers is like a yardstick, marked every inch. With that, the scaler measured the log's diameter. The numbers underneath the 4-inch mark (10, 12, 14, 16, and 18) represent log lengths in feet. Once the scaler knew the diameter and length of a log, he could read the board footage by following the appropriate row and column until they met. For example, a 16-foot log with an 8-inch diameter measured 44 board feet of lumber.

Two men were needed to use a crosscut saw. One pulled the saw toward him. Then the man on the opposite side of the tree pulled it back. After just two to three minutes, the tree fell toward the undercut, or notch.

Logging tools remained simple for many years. New Englanders liked the heavy axes they had developed during their masting days. Crosscut saws appeared in the mid-1800s, but they did not replace axes for another fifty years or so. By then, sharpening methods were improved, better quality steel was being manufactured, and raker teeth had been added to the saw blade to clean out sawdust with every stroke. With a sharp crosscut saw, a 20-inch (51-centimeter) pine could be felled in a couple of minutes after the undercut was chopped. Crosscuts were used until the chain saw became common after World War II.

The one tool essential to all logging operations was the peavey, or improved cant dog. It revolutionized lumbering. Invented in 1858 by Joseph Peavey, a blacksmith from Stillwater, Maine, it was used by loading crews at yards and landings and on river drives. A heavy 5- to 6-foot (1.5- to 2-meter) handle had a spike on the end, and a dog, or hook, that looked like half a pair of tongs. With it, a logger could stick the spike into a log, grab the log with the hook, and roll it. First used in the local Penobscot area, it quickly spread. When Maine loggers moved westward, they took it with them. It became the standard logging tool across America for one hundred years. Most Mainers called it a cant dog, but in other areas it was—and still is—known as a peavey.

At first, trees were cut and hauled directly to landings, near streams. About the time of the Civil War, men began to cut farther away from streams, so logs were twitched to yards near the cutting site. By midwinter, cutting stopped. A yarding crew loaded logs onto "two-sleds" and teams of horses hauled them from the yards

Some horses became so accustomed to twitching logs, they needed no teamster to guide them. They followed the twitching trail to the yard. There, someone unhitched the log and sent the horse back for more.

to the landing. There the logs were piled, either on a riverbank or out onto a frozen pond.

Oxen were used in the woods until the late 1800s. Oxen were nowhere near as excitable as horses, but horses could pull many more logs in a day. So, by mid-century, horses outnumbered oxen in the woods, and by 1890 oxen were replaced.

A draft horse weighs up to a ton. Smaller horses could be used for twitching, but heavy teams were needed for hauling loads of logs and for toting supplies. All winter the horses wore shoes with calks (spikes) in them to grip the ice. Horses' harnesses had bells on them so crews could hear a team approaching. Heavy four-horse tote teams had the right-of-way. Teamsters could tell one another from a distance by the distinctive tones of their jingle bells.

One of the coldest, loneliest jobs in a logging operation was icing down the roads. A four-horse team had to pull the sprinkler wagon over every hauling road—in the middle of the night, when the temperature was coldest. The team pulled a sled with a huge tank on it, which held about forty barrels of water. In the back of the tank, just over the sled runners, were two holes with plugs in them. Teamsters drove the horses slowly down the road. Wherever they wanted ice, they unplugged the holes and water dripped out into the sled ruts. Going down hills, they plugged the holes, so ice would *not* form. Night after night this frigid procedure had to be done, until hauling was over for the season.

Crews worked hard to keep hills free of ice, so loaded sleds would not speed up too much going down hills. On gentle slopes, teamsters wrapped bridle chains around the runners for brakes.

Hay was spread on some downhill grades to hold sleds back, and on the steepest hills a snub line was used. Despite all that, many horse teams ran out of control going down a hill and tipped the load over. "Getting sluiced," the men called it. Whole teams, including the teamsters, were killed.

Northern New England has some brutally cold spells—sometimes -30°F (-34.4°C) for weeks at a time. No matter how cold it got, loggers logged. There were rare exceptions—like in December 1890 when the temperature fell to -64°F (-53.3°C) in Aroostook County, Maine. No wonder loggers refused to work!

It took a four-horse team to pull the heavy sprinkler wagon. Every night, in temperatures well below zero, a team iced all the logging roads.

The cutting season lasted only a few months. An early snow cover could add weeks to logging operations. But if it came before ponds froze, the ponds did not freeze solidly enough. Too much snow was a problem for choppers. It was a lot more work to chop a tree down when they had to shovel 7 or 8 feet (2.1 or 2.4 meters) of snow just to get to it. On the other hand, too little snow meant an early breakup of ice on lakes and rivers. Warm, sunny days of March made snow roads mushy. If that happened too fast, teamsters couldn't haul all the logs to the landing before the spring runoff.

Logging is one of the most dangerous jobs there is. Nationwide, the accident rate among loggers has always been high compared to other industries. Horrible accidents occurred in the woods. Woodsmen were killed when struck on the head by a falling tree. Legs and arms were cut off or dislocated or broken. A chopper's ax sometimes slipped, driving into his leg instead of the tree. One wrong move at a yard or landing could make the whole pile of logs come crashing down. Men, horses, sleds—whatever was in the way—got crushed. New methods of harvesting trees are much safer. Still, logging remains one of the most hazardous occupations in America.

Facing page: With sled runners in front, a team of horses could drag several logs at once. Note the teamster's cant dog jabbed into one of the top logs. He will use that to roll the logs off at the landing.

A CHOPPER

It's 5:00 A.M. "ROLL OUT!" the cookee yells into the bunkhouse. You, and dozens of others, groan. But if you don't get up, Moose will be blazin' mad. He's the head chopper and he means to cut wood. Your heavy pants and wool socks didn't quite dry overnight, but you put them on anyway.

"Don't bother to splash your face this mornin'," you yell to the others. "There's thick ice in the pail again."

It's still dark when you finish eating breakfast, but you grab your ax, the crosscut, a half dozen fresh doughnuts from the barrel, and head into the woods. The snow squeaks as you walk along. By the time you get to the logging site, the sun is coming up. Every daylight moment counts, according to Moose.

The head chopper always scarfs the trees. Old Moose can make the smoothest undercut you ever saw. He knows how to land a tree exactly where he wants it. He makes the undercut so the tree will fall with its butt toward the hauling road. "Don't want a hoss to have to turn around just to twitch 'er out to the yard," he says.

Moose stands with his feet wide apart. Whack! He swings his ax into that tree with a magnificent wallop. Every few seconds, another huge chip flies out.

"OK, you two," he says a moment later. "Grab that misery whip, and take 'er down."

You and Pierre pick up the crosscut saw. Your bodies sway back and forth in steady rhythm, and the saw spews out long curls of sawdust. When the saw starts to "pinch," you pound a wedge into the cut to spread it open a little. Then you and Pierre go at it again. Before long, you roll your shirt sleeves up, you're sweating so much. And it's 20° below zero!

Pierre pulls a pop bottle from his pants pocket. "Mets p'tit bit kerosene on saw," he says. "Keep away pitch, for saw fast."

As always, when a tree begins to shake, Moose warns the rest of the crew to back off. "You don't wanna be in the way if she kicks back on the stump," he says.

"TIMBERRR!" The tree crackles inside, then crashes to the ground. Your insides crackle a little, too.

For a second, you watch the old-timers munch on frozen wood ants that fall out of the pine. But Moose won't let you stand there long. You and Pierre limb it and buck it into five 16-footers. Then you go to another tree and start all over. The teamster will be back soon with a horse to twitch the logs away, one at a time.

Shortly before noon, the cookee comes by with tins full of hot lunch, but it's so cold today nobody sits down to eat. You gulp down the baked beans, a fistful of biscuits, and drink some hot tea.

When the boss comes by to look things over, he brings news. "Ham Bone's gone for a while," he says. "The tote team's luggin' him to old Doc Sawbones. Fifty miles! Gorry, is he mad!" Yesterday he chopped his big toe off when he was limbing. Way the devil out here, in the middle of nowhere, and they had to sled him back to camp. Old Ham Bone screamed bloody murder when the boss yanked his boot off and bandaged his foot the best he could.

The scaler comes around to count your logs. He about freezes to death waiting for logs to be cut. He keeps jumping up and down to keep his toes from going numb.

The sky's purple when you head back to camp. After supper you sharpen your ax on the grindstone. You're glad it's Pierre's turn to sharpen the crosscut.

The scaler posts everybody's tally in the bunkhouse. You did better today. "All right!" says Moose, slapping you on the back. "You'll be a top-notch woodsman in no time."

You spread your socks and shirt on the woodpile. With everyone's clammy clothes around the fire, the whole bunkhouse steams with wet wool and sweat.

Now, after pulling a crosscut all day, you're ready to hit the bunk. 5:00 A.M. comes early.

A Day in the Life of...

A TEAMSTER

As usual you're up at 4:30 A.M. to feed and care for your horses. They need to wait a while after eating before they can go to work.

"Thirty below this mornin'," says the cookee.

"Never mind the thermometer," grumbles Zeke, the head teamster. "We're hookin' up the two-sleds. Time's gettin' short." He turns to you and says, "You better be good with a four-hoss team, 'cause if all them piles of logs ain't down by the river when the ice goes out, you're mincemeat."

Up to now, you've been twitching logs to the yard with one, sometimes two, horses. Day after day, for weeks, you've barely kept up with the choppers.

While you are harnessing up, Zeke keeps talking. "It's a three-turn road," he says, adding plenty of swear words. "That means you should be able t' make three trips a day from yard to landing and back. Ya hear? And watch them slopes," he adds. "If them hosses gits hurt, you're headin' downriver."

He's a cussed old teamster, all right, but you have never seen him treat his horses mean. He never whips them hard or kicks them, like some teamsters do.

Chains and bells jingle as you head out of camp. It's still dark and so cold you can hardly breathe. Your horses snort clouds of frost as they clop along.

You're glad you listened to Zeke when he told you to wear lots of clothes. It takes almost an hour to load your two-sled at the yard. You put blankets over your horses.

With their cant dogs, the yarding crew rolls those logs onto the sled bunks, each log thudding as it drops on.

You climb atop your pile of logs. "Giddyap!" The runner tracks are so slick, your horses pull the heavy load at a decent clip on the level. On slight down-grades, you drop your bridle chains to brake slightly.

"Whooooaaa!" Here on this steep grade, you hook up to the snub machine, set its brake, and head down. They had simple snub lines long ago when they were hauling mast trees out of here. You're glad they're steel cables now. Still, sometimes they break. Your whole team could be buried under tons of long logs! But you make it this time, take a deep breath, and haul up to the landing.

Returning with your empty sled, you listen. If you hear another team's bells, you must get off at a turnout, and let it pass. Loaded sleds have the right-of-way.

You stop where you dropped the feed bags of oats and hay this morning and allow your horses an hour to eat. You can eat in five or ten minutes, but they can't. You unhook their bridles and let them munch away.

Each time you stop at a yard or landing, you check for snowballs. Horses' calked shoes get all balled up with snow, so you grab the hammer that's hanging from the harness and knock the snow off.

Stars are out when you return to camp. Your horses snort as they trudge along, heads nodding. They know they're headed home. Back at the hovel, there is still work to do before you can eat supper.

You rub your horses down, put their blankets on, and feed and water them. Their fetlocks are caked with ice, so you wrap them in burlap strips. The ice melts while you eat supper, then you unwind the burlap and dry your horses' legs with rags. You nuzzle up to each horse for a moment, then crawl into your bunk in the corner of the hovel. As you douse the lantern, you hear Zeke mutter, "You got a good way with them hosses, kid. You'll do OK."

Chapter 4

BACK AT CAMP

*The bunkhouse reeked!
Wet wool socks drying,
wood smoke, smelly
men. No sheets on the
beds, only blankets.
Men slept in their long
johns, and sometimes
they didn't take 'em off
for weeks!*

*Albert Soule
Scaler/Clerk, Camp 12
Crystal, New Hampshire,
1941*

Crude logging camps appeared deep in the woods in the early 1800s. In the earliest ones, men built a one-room cabin and a hovel. The dirt floor at one end of the cabin was the bed. Hay or hemlock boughs made the mattress. The whole crew, maybe a dozen men, slept under one blanket, which was made from two quilts sewn together and stuffed with straw. If anyone wanted a pillow, he rolled up his coat. Even though the quilt stuffing got bug infested, the quilt was not washed all winter. Men were packed in so tightly, if a man wanted to turn over, he yelled, "Flop!" and everybody turned at once.

Each night men stoked an open fire in the middle of the dirt floor, to lend a little warmth through the night. If the fire burned too low, cold air came through the open chimney, which was a hole in the roof, and the men nearly froze. Sometimes the camp caught fire, but most often someone discovered it and threw snow or water on it before the camp burned down. Occasionally the crew burned to death.

Every camp, from the very earliest lumbering days, had a deacon seat, made from one half of a long spruce log, with stick legs. At first, it served as a table, too. The crew ate lots of pickled beef and boiled codfish right out of the cook pot. A hollowed log made

A good cook was an absolute must in a logging camp. Woodsmen expected good food—and lots of it! Cookees waited on tables and washed dishes.

a kitchen sink. The only other piece of furniture was a grindstone for sharpening axes.

The ox hovel had a wooden floor, so the animals' tender hooves could be kept off the frozen ground when they were not working. There was a place for hay storage, too. Teamsters usually bunked in the hovel with the animals.

By the mid-nineteenth century, double camps were being built. The cooking area and the sleeping quarters were at opposite ends of a long building, with a dingle in between, kind of like a breeze-way with a back wall. A few bulky supplies were kept there. Windows were added, floors were put in, bunk beds were built, and cast-iron stoves were introduced. Camps even began hiring cooks and providing tables, tin cups and plates, and silverware.

Later in the century, the boss got separate quarters, a clerk was hired, and a wangan, or company store, was added. *Wangan* is an American Indian word that means "camping place." By 1900 many camps had a blacksmith shop, an office, and a filer's and teamster's shack. Most were crudely built and covered with tar paper, because logging companies intended to use them for only a few years.

As lumber camps grew larger, more and more supplies were needed. Can you imagine 50,000 barrels of flour, 6,000 barrels of pork, plus lots of other food for the winter? In addition, thousands of bushels of oats were needed for the animals.

Men could buy warm woolen clothing at the company store. They also bought chewing tobacco, liniment for their sore muscles, and a few other items.

Men cut fir boughs to soften their log bunks. Some men cut fresh boughs often, both to get more softness and to get rid of the lice living in the bed.

The outhouse improved by 1900. Five-holers had fancy toilet paper by then—*Farmer's Almanac* or *Sears, Roebuck* catalogs. Men could rip off a page at a time and get almost through the catalog by spring! Not that they would want to sit there and read catalogs. Some outhouses still had open fronts, and all were well ventilated— and temperatures were below zero much of the time! But it beat the earlier two-pole system, "one to sit on and one to lean against."

Lumbermen lived in the large bunkhouse. Men could shave at the sink in a corner near the door, but few bothered. It was much too cold to bathe. Besides, they covered themselves with liniment all winter. That, and gobs of talcum powder to keep lice away. A few kerosene lanterns hung at the foot of the men's bunks. Around the woodstove in the middle of the room was a rack for drying socks and mittens. Logging camps had a dank odor. Wet, woolen socks were stinky enough, but teamsters added horse sweat to the mix when they brought harnesses in to dry on the woodpile.

In some large logging camps built in the early 1900s, families arrived. Little houses were built for the boss's, cook's, blacksmith's, and perhaps the scaler's families. Occasionally women were cooks, and a few large operations even hired teachers and ran one-room schools.

After World War I, camps became more comfortable and sanitary. Individual beds replaced bunks, but the traditional deacon seat stayed. A little later a few camps had electric lights. Organizations provided reading materials. Eventually, even in remote woods camps, telephones and radios were available and, for a short time, television. But by the late 1950s, automobiles had such

Beginning in the early 1900s, some families moved into lumber camps. This young boy hauls small logs in his make-believe logging operation. His pony-size logging sled was made by the camp blacksmith. The young boy shown here is the author's father.

easy access into logging operations, there really was no need for lumber camps anymore.

The severe cold was a nuisance. It was almost impossible to keep warm in temperatures well below zero. Lumbermen wore red wool underwear, heavy pants, one or two wool shirts, a heavy mackinaw, a wool cap, two or more pairs of wool socks inside their leather-topped boots, and two pairs of mitts—all at once!

Their biggest nuisance was bugs. No lumber camps were free from lice and bedbugs. Everyone got lousy. Bugs invaded everywhere—even the seams of the men's underwear. Men could get temporary relief if they hung their bedding around the camp and burned sulfur for several hours to fumigate the bunkhouse.

There was little illness in logging camps, despite the squalid living conditions. Subzero temperatures killed most bacteria. There were one or two outbreaks of smallpox, but in the twentieth century, vaccinations took care of that scare. Lumbermen rubbed salt pork on cuts and bruises. Their hands got so dried and cracked and bloody, they sewed them up with needle and thread. Accidents, of course, were their biggest problems.

Loggers didn't protest against their crude living conditions. They were as well off as many rural Americans. They would protest, though, if food was not good. Loggers ate more than any other workers anywhere. After the Civil War, baked beans replaced dried codfish and salt pork as the staple food. Not long after, in the 1890s, lumber companies began to compete for crews by the food they provided. Beans and brown bread still appeared at every meal, but menus became much more varied.

A good cook kept a logging crew happy. Before daylight each day, the cook baked bread, pies, doughnuts, and more. To cook for one hundred men, he used two-thirds of a barrel of flour every day. That is as much as twenty-six 5-pound (2.3-kilogram) bags of flour. The cook was lord of the cookshack, and everybody knew it! Even the boss did not interfere! The cook also administered first aid and wrote letters for those who could not write.

Cooks' helpers, cookees, did the menial chores around the dining hall and bunkhouse. Young, unskilled woodsmen often hired in as cookees, many seventeen or eighteen years old. They washed dishes, scrubbed floors, cut and split wood, built fires, lugged water, and fed the pigs. They peeled vegetables, kneaded dough, and learned to cook. They helped serve meals and carried lunches to the men working in the woods.

At dinner a new man had to wait until everyone was seated, then take a leftover seat. Men sat in the same seat every meal. One strict rule was no talking while eating, except "Please" or "Thank you." Some say it was so men would eat quickly and get out. Others say it was so men would not start fighting. Whatever the reason, the custom prevailed in logging camps all over the country.

The blacksmith's hours were long, his work hard. In addition to shoeing all the horses, he made sled runners, axheads, nails, and every kind of tool—even coffins. And, of course, something was always in need of repair or replacement—sleds, chains, and more. Besides everything else, he was often an amateur veterinarian. In small outfits, teamsters doubled as blacksmiths.

Lumberjack Cookies

This recipe was written on the back of an old brown bag.

1 cup lard	2 tsp. salt
1 cup butter	2 tsp. soda
2 cups sugar	3 tsp. baking powder
3 cups raisins	1 tsp. cream of tartar
1 cup milk	1/2 tsp. nutmeg
6 cups flour	1/2 tsp. cloves
1 cup molasses	1/2 tsp. ginger
2 cups oatmeal	1/2 tsp. cinnamon
4 eggs	2 tbsp. vanilla

Sift dry ingredients together. Mix in liquids. Roll out 1/4 inch and cut with cutter for oven, or roll out as above and fry in hot skillet—like fritters. Or drop raw dough in deep fat and cook like doughnuts. Or drop gobs of dough on pan and bake as drop cookies.

Taken from the book, *It Happened Up in Maine*, by Benjamin C. Cole (courtesy of Lumbermen's Museum, Patten, Maine).

Saw filers kept crosscut saws sharp. Dull saws did not cut well. They were not safe, and using them wasted time, energy, and money. So, nearly every logging operation hired a saw filer. Loggers nicknamed him Old Squint Eye, for he often strained his eyes working all day sharpening and setting sawteeth.

The camp clerk lived in the camp office, with the boss and the scaler. That's also where he worked. He ordered the camp's supplies and kept payroll ledgers. Every night the scaler reported the day's "scale" totals for every logger. It was the clerk's job to add up everyone's "thousands" each week. That's thousands of board feet cut, not dollars. After deducting the price of anything purchased at the store that week, the clerk paid the men—but not in money. Instead, a man earned credit. Actual payment came when camp broke up in the spring. Keeping all those records earned the clerk the nickname Inkslinger. He also sorted mail and helped the cookee cut firewood for the camp. In some camps, the scaler doubled as the clerk.

Loggers worked hard six days a week. On Saturday night, they danced and sang for hours. Someone would fiddle, and men danced the jigs of their native lands—Canada, Ireland, Finland, Norway, Sweden, England, Scotland, Russia, and Poland. There was much singing. Men made up long ballads about loggers and river drivers and their legendary feats. A good singer could entertain a crowd for hours. Tale spinners dreamed up hilarious tall tales. Contests and games, such as poker, sometimes lasted all winter. The legend of giant logger Paul Bunyan was not known in Maine lumber camps, but he appeared in the Great Lakes area before 1900.

Who were these loggers? Legend would have us believe they were society's outcasts, tough and unruly, drunken bums. True, a fair percentage of them did kick up their heels when they came out of the woods in the spring, but in camps liquor was forbidden. They were men of all ages from many cultural traditions. Most had little education, and a large number could not read or write. They tended to be rough, but many were skilled craftsmen. All took great pride in their work, and they showed a remarkable sense of humor. Some legendary lumbermen showed a flair for daring and adventure, but most were ordinary citizens trying to eke out a living for their families. Regardless, while in the woods, these men worked. Like beasts of burden! Too many sacrificed their lives. Under grueling conditions, they sweated and strained to meet the boss's command, "Get out that timber!"

A COOKEE

It's 4:00 A.M. You get a crackling fire going in the woodstove. The cook needs to bake a dozen or more loaves of bread and hundreds of rolls, plus fry a bushel of doughnuts.

"Meow," says Mousetrap, as she moseys by. She's been up all night, feasting in the storeroom and out in the hovel.

You wash and stew prunes before waking the crew at 5:00. Then you make sure tables are ready. At 5:30 you bang the gong, just outside the door. "COME AND GET IT!"

Men pile in and start reaching for the food you have placed on each table—sausage, baked beans, biscuits, oatmeal, stewed prunes, and a heap of other things. The men gulp down their food and carry their dishes to the sink. Plates go in one washtub, silverware in the other. Food scraps go into a barrel, for you to feed to the pigs. In just fifteen minutes, they have eaten and are gone.

Before you finish washing the dishes, the cook orders, "Get to peeling those potatoes. We need a bushel for supper tonight. These old hoptoads eat somethin' scandalous." You peel potatoes while he makes about twenty pies.

It's just you and the cook in the kitchen most of the time during the day. The fact is, nobody dares to set foot inside the cook's kingdom, except for mealtime. Only the boss, the scaler, and the clerk—and the blacksmith's children. Every day they peek around the doorway, you give each of them a molasses cookie, and they scamper off to play.

It seems as if you have to do all the dirty jobs around here. Wash dishes. Wipe tables. Sweep floors. Haul water. Lug firewood. Fill kettles. One chore after another, all day long. The clerk helps you cut firewood for the stoves. Keeping fires going all day is a nagging chore.

By late morning you pack the loggers' lunch onto a sled and haul it into the woods. Tooter, one of the old-timers, has a fire blazing, so you heat water for tea. "Food's freezin' right ont' these blessed tin plates," he

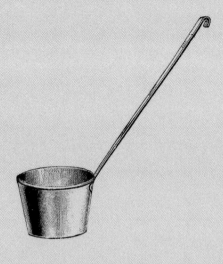

growls. After he scoffs down his beans and biscuits, he adds, "A bit stingy with the 'super-sinkers' today, aren't ya? You feedin' that bear agin?" Everyone knows there are plenty of doughnuts, but these geezers like to josh. They will never stop teasing you about the night a bear got into the storehouse and tipped over the molasses barrel. "That old critter was lappin' up our molasses somethin' fierce," Tooter's been saying for a week now. You laugh with them, remembering Old Tooter and a bunch of others standing there in their red long johns in the middle of the night, banging kettles and whooping and hollering like crazy. Now you make sure the latch is secure every time you leave the storeroom.

Back in the kitchen, you boil and mash potatoes. You set the tables as always, with enameled tin plates and bowls upside down at each man's place.

BONG, BONG, BONG. You call the men to supper.

From the moment the men sit down, you are replenishing beans, tea, and biscuits. One brute starts grumbling about the food. After arguing with the man next to him, he hollers out, "What the devil did you do to these beans?"

The cook grabs him by the scruff of the neck. "See that sign?" he roars. NO TALKING. *NE PARLEZ PAS.* "Gripe out there!" he shouts, throwing the man out the door.

At the end of the meal, you're back at the sink again. There are more dishes to wash after the last teamsters get in, long after dark.

You stoke the fires in the woodstoves, and order "Lights Out!" at 9:00 P.M.

A WOODSMAN

"What's the matter, PeeWee?" you say. "Got Blanket Fever?" PeeWee grunts and turns over. He's lazy today.

Last night, the New Brunswickers started their step dance. They roused everyone in camp and divided you all in pairs, facing each other. You faced PeeWee, and every step he did, you had to imitate. He had you kicking and high-stepping until you were all out of breath. What a hullabaloo!

PeeWee doesn't care if he skips Sunday breakfast. It is the only day you don't have to get up at 5:00 A.M. But you want to cut fresh balsam boughs for a new mattress. While you're out gathering boughs, you find some spruce gum, the "goo" that oozes out of wounds on a spruce tree. After you chew your wad for a while, it tastes good.

You pat down your fresh bough bed, then shake some talcum powder around. "Trying to get rid of them hard-shelled old grandfathers?" asks PeeWee, still lying in bed. "Them bedbugs will be back in a couple o' days, no matter what you do."

Every Sunday, you change underwear, and wash clothes in a cauldron outside. You boil your long johns to kill the lice, so you won't itch too much for a few days.

At the wangan, a lot of loggers buy liniment for their aching shoulders, and just about everyone buys a can of chewing tobacco.

René is giving haircuts. He lops off wads of your hair, lice and all.

Some men have gone deer hunting, others ice fishing, or snowshoeing.

The teamsters are in the hovel grooming horses, oiling harnesses, and mending horse blankets.

You mend a rip in your wool shirt, then you grease your leather-top boots. Last Sunday, you found a nice piece of white ash wood, so you whittle on your new ax handle for a while.

It's a motley crew up here in the woods. Some of these old geezers have more ideas than the cook has beans. Some sit around playing cards. Most of the men cannot read, but they like to sit around the stove and tell stories. PeeWee tells his favorite story about a lousy blanket that walks across the floor and trips up the boss. He's told it so many times, you'd like to take a cant dog to him.

Big Burly starts singing one of his river driving songs, adding more and more verses to the story. "Twas on a Sunday mornin,' . . ." On and on he blares. Everybody's off key, but you all enjoy bellowing out the choruses.

One of the Frenchmen starts playing his harmonica and René begins, *"Alouette, gentille Alouette. . ."* He gets everybody going, stamping feet and shouting verses. The deacon seats are crowded with guys stamping like crazy.

Most Sundays you have contests. There's always a poker tournament going on, with tobacco as stakes.

Today's feature contest is the big louse race. Big Burly and PeeWee have been picking lice from their armpit hair, choosing the biggest one. All week, men have been betting on whose louse will crawl the length of the newspaper first! Ready, set, off they go! Big Burly's louse is streaking along. Here comes PeeWee's. "Yea! Go, PeeWee!" you shout. The cookee's out in the cookshack, roaring with laughter.

Chapter 5

GOING DOWN WITH THE DRIVE

. . . long logs—well, they come surging down the current like express trains, shedding green water from their backs, and leaping over boulders. There's something vicious about their bulk and speed—something alive and dangerous.

Louise Dickinson Rich
We Took to the Woods,
1942

Once trees were cut, there was just one way to get them to sawmills—float them down rivers. Logs could be rafted and poled down many rivers in America, but New England's are too rough. Logs had to be driven. When the winter snows melted, the spring runoff, or freshet, began to flow out of the mountains. The drive was on! Sometimes it took until fall to get those logs to sawmills.

Logging was so profitable in the mid-nineteenth century, men got greedy for logs. To get more lumber, they found ways to divert water from one river system into another. Several attempts were made over the years to change water flow.

The river drive was the most dangerous part of logging. New England rivers are full of rapids and ledges. Men could easily be washed over falls or swept over a dam. Drivers were crushed when a log jam let go. More men were killed from capsized bateaux than from any other cause. Sometimes a man's body was found several miles downriver from where he went under. But the drive went on.

River drivers worked in numbing cold, seven days a week, dawn to dark. Standing up to their armpits in icy water, they dragged logs over rocks and ledges. Ice chunks bruised their bodies, their feet swelled and cracked from being wet so long at a time. It was miserable work.

Log jams were common on river drives. Here more than a dozen men poke at logs with their cant dogs to start the logs moving downriver again.

This expert river driver balances on a log heading downriver. He holds his cant dog ready to use at a second's notice.

"River hogs," as they were often called, wore special driving boots. They had steel spikes in the soles, called calks, to keep the men from slipping on rolling logs and wet rocks.

Drivers used a cumbersome cant dog with a hook that swung every which way, until Joseph Peavey improved it. Peavey's new "dog" (hook) swung up and down, but not back and forth, so it was easier to clamp onto a log. The tool was used to roll logs off landings into streams, and to pry logs loose from rocks or riverbanks. The other essential tool was a pickpole, or pike pole. It was a long pole 12 to 16 feet (4 to 5 meters) with a screwlike spike at the end.

Bateaux were heavy, flat-bottomed boats with flared sides—a distinctive feature of north woods river driving. They varied from 25 to 35 feet (8 to 11 meters) long and were used for more than two centuries on Maine's rocky, twisting rivers. The prow extended out 6 or 7 feet (1.8 to 2 meters), so a man could jump ashore without the boat having to land. And a bateau could pick a man up quickly from a mass of logs, critical when escaping a log jam. It took six men to maneuver the biggest bateaux, for they weighed 800 to 900 pounds (363 to 409 kilometers).

Elaborate dam systems evolved to hold the water back until the drive boss released it. Holding dams controlled large amounts of water. When the gates were opened, men worked feverishly to keep logs moving, then dropped the gates to save water. Roll dams were smaller. Logs could roll right over them on a high pitch of water. Splash dams held back water in small streams long enough for the drive to go through, then were removed. Men built sluiceways and canals in the toughest spots.

When logs from different tributaries reached the main river, a million or more logs were mixed together. Rivers got so crowded, log driving companies were formed to coordinate the drives. Logging operators paid tolls to use the river. The money helped build and repair dams, sluiceways, and booms. Boom corporations were organized to sort each logging operation's logs at the end of the drives. The Androscoggin River had a boom as early as 1789. The Kennebec Boom Corporation was formed in 1795. In 1835 the Penobscot Boom Company had an elaborate string of sorting booms, 2 miles (3.2 kilometers) long and holding up to 600 acres (243 hectares) of logs.

The master driver decided when to start the drive. Water level was critical. Too much water would strand logs on riverbanks, too little would hang up logs on rocks in mid-river. On a good flow, logs could travel about 2 miles (3.2 kilometers) per hour. The boss drove his men like demons, for the "spring freshets" did not last long. If the drive did not reach sawmills while there was water enough, it would be "hung" until the next spring. A "hung" drive was not only a disgrace, it meant no pay!

All logs piled along the riverbanks were peeled off into the river. That process took up to a week. Logs usually had to be prodded with peavey and pickpole. Sometimes, however, releasing one log started an avalanche of logs tumbling into the water. Any riverman caught in the way was crushed to death. If woodsmen had piled the logs on frozen ponds or lakes, they were in a "boom," a circle of logs chained end to end. Rivermen pulled the boom to the head of the pond, and shoved the logs downstream.

Long boats, called bateaux, were used on New England river drives. This bateau is carrying river drivers out into the river to work on a log jam.

Keeping long logs moving downriver was tough and dangerous work.

Rivermen "tended out" along the shore. Whenever logs caught on rocks or sandbars or snagged on bushes along the banks, men rushed into the river to poke them along. If they did not work quickly, jams piled up.

Every few days, camp would move 10 to 15 miles (16 to 24 kilometers) downriver. The wangan, or supply outfit, toted everything for eating and sleeping. Once the drive reached the main river, two or three bateaux were used. Sleeping quarters were two lean-tos, facing each other, with about 6 feet (2 meters) between them, where two fireplaces were built. Most drives had four meals a day. Breakfast was at 4:00 A.M.; supper, whenever they got in at night. Cookees carried two lunches to the men along the river; first lunch about 9:00 or 10:00 A.M., second lunch at 2:00 P.M. Men on the Androscoggin drive ate five meals a day, with an extra lunch at noon.

When logs reached a lake, they had to be towed to the other end. Thousands of logs were corralled inside a huge boom made of long logs chained together, end to end. The boom was attached to a raft called a headworks. In the center of the headworks stood a huge spool with spokes at the top, called a capstan. Attached to the capstan was a long, heavy rope, with a 300-pound (136-kilogram) anchor at the other end. The anchor was rowed out ahead by bateau and dropped. Men wound the rope around the capstan, pulling the raft and all the logs up to the anchor. This process was repeated over and over for twelve or more hours a day. Men walked around and around, pushing the spokes, sometimes half asleep. They had to step over the rope once each time around. Occasionally, a man would trip, fall overboard, and drown. Meals were brought from shore. Often they towed at night, after winds

Men sweated long and hard to tow logs along lakes. They trudged in circles on a raft called a headworks for up to twelve hours at a time. Finally, by the 1890s, steamboats replaced manpower.

CHANGING COURSES

In the 1830s lumbermen looked for ways to increase their profits. That meant driving more logs. One way to do that was to change the natural course of water from one drainage basin to another. Moosehead Lake, Maine's largest, flows out the Kennebec River. Its north cove is less than 2 miles (3.2 kilometers) from the Penobscot River system. In 1839, Kennebec lumbermen proposed a sluiceway to divert logs into Moosehead and down the Kennebec. Bangor's lumber barons protested, so the project was dropped. It was more than fifty years later when a conveyor system was built in that area, and it was used for only a few years. One conveyor pulled Penobscot logs up, dumped them onto a second conveyor, and sent them down a 2-mile (3.2-kilometer)-long sluiceway to Kennebec waters.

Penobscot lumbermen wanted more timber, too. The Allagash River flows deep in the wilderness of northern Maine. It is a tributary of the St. John River, which flows into Canada and empties into the Bay of Fundy. Separating the two watersheds was a ravine, less than a mile long, between Telos Lake and Webster Lake, 45 feet (14 meters) lower. In 1841 dams were built to raise Chamberlain Lake to Telos's level and regulate waterflow. Then a canal was cut between Telos and Webster lakes, and Allagash water gushed down into the Penobscot watershed. The canal, called the Telos Cut, opened in the spring of 1842. Conflicts followed for years, but millions of pine and spruce logs came into Bangor instead of Canada. The Telos Cut caused so much trouble, in fact, the conflict was called the Telos War.

In 1903, a tramway was built to bring still more Allagash logs to Penobscot mills—out of Eagle Lake into Chamberlain Lake. A mile-long loop of steel cable went around two pulleys; one underwater in Eagle Lake, the other above water at Chamberlain. Little trucks on narrow gauge railroad tracks straddled the cable. Logs, one on each truck, were pulled up the long rise by steam power, and dumped into Chamberlain Lake. The Eagle Lake Tramway ran for about six years.

died down. A lantern on the raft and bonfires on shore lit their way. This towing process took days and days. It sometimes took two weeks to reach the end of the longest lakes, such as 18-mile (29-kilometer)-long Chesuncook Lake on the west branch of the Penobscot River. A sudden storm could snap the boom and scatter logs all over the lake. That could cause delay of a year or more before logs reached the sawmills. Finally, steamboats were introduced and the horrid process of towing by hand was over.

Logs often jammed going downriver. All it took was for one log to get caught, and others would pile on top of it. River crews patrolled dawn to dark, trying to keep the logs moving. Still, some log jams got so enormous, they blocked an entire river for a half mile (.8 kilometer). In 1881, one jam at Caratunk Falls on the Kennebec was a mile long (1.6 kilometers) and 100 feet (30 meters) high! When a jam formed, word was relayed upriver to stop putting logs into the water. In the 1890s telephone lines were strung along some rivers, which helped. Hand-crank phones were nailed to trees every 5 to 6 miles (8 to 10 kilometers).

It took hours or days or even weeks to break a jam. Men picked logs loose with their cant dogs and pickpoles if they could. Sometimes chopping the "key log" off would start logs rolling again. In deep gorges, men were lowered by ropes to chop the key log. Sometimes they were yanked up in time. Sometimes they weren't. When a jam "hauled," or let loose, men scrambled for shore. If they could not make it, they rode one of the logs down through the rapids. Some were thrown into the water. The most nimble rivermen became known as Bangor Tigers. If nothing else freed a jam, the drive boss blasted it with dynamite.

Some log jams had to be blasted with dynamite to start logs moving downriver again.

Men used long pickpoles to sort millions of logs at sorting booms.

After the main drive went down, the river crew rounded up the logs that got stuck behind rocks or riverbanks and sent them downstream. It was often late September before they finished. "Sacking the rear," as they called it, was nasty work—not the most dangerous, but physically grueling.

Finally the drive reached its end at the sorting booms, just upriver from the sawmills. There, logs were separated by their log marks. Rafts of sorted logs were held until sawmill owners purchased them from the logging operations that cut them months earlier.

River drives became less important as trucks and railroads hauled more and more logs. New England's longest river, the Connecticut, held its last long-log drive in 1915. Long logs were driven down the Androscoggin River until 1930. Penobscot logs floated downriver until about that time, too. Long logs were driven down the Saco River from the early eighteenth century until 1947. The Machias River ran log drives longer than any other river—from Revolutionary War days until the mid-1960s. After long-log drives disappeared, paper companies continued to drive 4-foot (1.2-meter) pulpwood logs. Finally, it was determined that logs polluted the rivers. Under pressure from environmentalists, the Maine legislature banned river drives after 1976. The river drive, sparked by the mast trade three centuries earlier, was over.

PULPWOOD DRIVES

In the early years of New England river driving, all logs were at least 12 feet (3.7 meters) long, and sometimes much longer—up to 50 or 60 feet (15 to 18 meters).

Early in the twentieth century, paper companies began running river drives, much different from the traditional long-log drives. They needed to grind logs into wood pulp to make paper, so they harvested short logs. In the woods, trees were cut into 4-foot (1.2 meters) lengths. Every spring, those logs crowded the rivers, but did not tend to form log jams. And, of course, river drivers could not walk on short logs. Drivers worked on shore or standing in bateaux. Paper companies held pulpwood drives for several years after long-log drives had ended, but eventually all logs were transported out of the woods by truck or railroad.

A RIVER DRIVER

"Can you ride on logs?"

"Sure," you tell the drive boss. He needs more men. And you need work.

"On the drive, days are longer than they were in the woods," he adds, "and the work's vicious. You'll be soakin' wet most o' the time. This ain't no Sunday school!"

You nod.

"And stag them trousers," he warns, "so's your boot calks don't catch."

You look around. All the men look shabby. And you realize all their pants are cut off just below the knees. One lanky guy, named Martti, stands there in his red wool shirt, his thumbs hooked on his grubby suspenders. He helps you stag your pants, then cuts a slit in the arch of your boots just above the sole. "Let ooze out water little bit," he says. "Feet all crack anyhow, but this help."

The boss has been watching the river for days. Today he roars, "ROLL 'EM!" Dozens of men start dumping logs from the landing into the stream. They lean into their cant dogs and roll logs at a furious pace.

"Tend out here," the drive boss barks at you and some others. "Don't want no logs jammin' up."

You're in and out of the water all morning, poking at logs to keep them flowing. If anyone sits down for a moment, the boss is yelling. "Don't you know how to roll a stick? Keep 'em movin'."

Martti helps you to shore after one long spell in the water. "Come. Rub legs and jump little bit around," he says. "Make blood to warm." In a few minutes, you head back into the icy stream.

The cookee lugs lunch to you twice during the day. Same meal, over and over—ham, potatoes, baked beans, bread, doughnuts, and strong tea. Just as you are gulping down your seventh doughnut, the boss yells again.

"See them logs startin' to jam by that bank?" he roars, pointing to the far shore. "Get 'em back int' the river, quick! Every damn one of 'em!"

You and four other river drivers jump into the

bateau, and the boatman takes you across. He pokes around logs and rocks with his pickpole. You five jump ashore and work feverishly, trudging waist-deep in icy water. You free a few logs with your cant dog.

"Jump in, NOW!" the boatman hollers.

Suddenly, sticks come tumbling over the rapids, crashing over one another, forming a pounding mass of logs. The boss waves furiously to someone upriver. "Stop the logs!" his arms say.

"Jee-e-e-roozlum!" he shrieks, swearing and stomping, before you're even back onshore. "We're gettin' a lulu of a jam here!"

The boss stares at the jam and yells, "We've gotta chop up that key log. Take turns. I don't want anyone gettin' all tuckered out," he says. "Gotta be able to make a beeline for shore faster 'n lightnin'."

After one river hog gets the notch started, you take your turn. "If you hear that log start to split," the boss says, "by Judas, you run like the bejeepers! When she hauls, she'll go tearin' like thunder!"

You make a few swings with your ax and get back safely, but that log mass is starting to rumble. Martti takes his turn next, chopping further into the key log. Before you can blink, the log snaps, releasing a geyser of water. The whole mass goes thrashing and grinding over the rapids, logs upending every which way. Martti can't get back! He leaps onto a log and starts riding it down through. He swivels and turns, dodging rocks like a pro. Suddenly his log rams into a boulder. Head over heels, he is thrown into the raging river.

"Damnation!" the boss cries. "Martti's gone down."

By the big rapids, you bury your buddy in his driving clothes, and hang his calked boots on a tree. He belongs here now. "He died doing his duty," the boss mutters. He scuffs some dirt onto the shallow grave.

Back at the wangan, the cook has a fire blazing and the big kettle boiling. Bread is baking in the Dutch ovens. You pick at your plate of beans and drink some hot tea. Then you crawl into the lean-to and plop onto the fir boughs. Some guys don't even take their boots off. Too stiff to put them on in the morning, they say.

All night long you hear the hollow thunk of logs bumping over the rapids. Like drums. In the morning you know you'll have more jams.

Sawmills were crowded along areas of rivers where dams could be made to provide adequate waterpower. These mills were along Kenduskeag Stream, a tributary of the Penobscot River in Maine.

Chapter 6

LOGS TO LUMBER

Frequently, and at the
least expected moment,
the working saw will
pick up a loose knot or
splinter from the log
and shoot it to the
extremity of the mill
with the velocity of a
rifle bullet.

George Woodbury
John Goffe's Mill, 1948

No one is certain when the first sawmill appeared in New England. Some claim as early as 1623, but we know there were sawmills operating in southernmost Maine by 1634 or 1635. Early sawmills served local areas primarily, and were usually gristmills and sawmills combined. Even the tiniest villages had a water-powered mill. Most sawmills were small, but they could produce at least five times as much lumber as men using pit saws.

By 1675 there were at least fifty water-powered sawmills in northern Massachusetts, New Hampshire, and Maine, each able to produce 500 to 1,000 board feet of white pine boards per day. Before many years, settlers had clapboard houses, rather than log homes, and large barns. The best pines, of course, were not sawed, but were sent to Britain. They belonged to the king.

By the time Maine became a state, in 1820, over seven hundred sawmills were operating. All had single, up-and-down saws, run by waterpower. With these saws, the log moved on a sliding carriage and the saw stayed in place.

The sawing season was limited to spring, summer, and fall, however, because of water flow. Some mills worked at night. They suffered from spring floods, summer droughts, and frozen winters, so they sat idle much of the time.

In the 1820s steam began to replace waterpower. Mills sped up. Steam mills had been operating in England before that, but they were not used here, because there was plenty of waterpower on New England's rivers, and logs could be floated directly to mills.

Early steam mills averaged 20 horsepower, had five to ten times the capacity of water-powered mills, and they could run year-round, except mud season and times of high fire danger. The steam engine meant sawmills were not tied to rivers anymore. They could be located almost anywhere. Even though steam engines were expensive to buy and operating costs were high, use of steam engines spread.

A 100-horsepower steam mill was built a few miles south of Bangor, Maine, in 1854. It could cut 60,000 board feet a day, working day and night. Within six years, Bangor had hundreds of sawmills, together producing more than 200 million board feet of lumber a year. Forty years earlier, water-powered mills were sawing barely one million board feet annually.

Other changes occurred in the middle of the nineteenth century. Gang saws became common. A gang saw is a row of up-and-down saws that work together on a single frame. Gang saws could saw an entire log into boards almost as quickly as a regular saw could saw a single board. Some gang saws had up to 24 blades. One company ran four gangs, side by side, totaling eighty-four saws! Gang saws cut timber to uniform dimensions. That was when the standard "2 x 4" became stock material for building houses. Gang saws are still used today.

Circular saws were patented in England in 1777. U.S. patents were issued in 1814 and 1820. There were two known circular

Steam-powered sawmills could be built away from rivers. This steam mill, located in northern New Hampshire, was built in the early 1900s. It was fueled by slabs of wood left over from the cut lumber. All winter, hardwood (such as birch, maple, hickory, and ash) was hauled to the landing behind the mill, which operated during the summer.

sawmills built in Maine in the 1820s, one on Kenduskeag Stream, near Bangor, and another in Waterville. Circular saws cut faster than other saws, but there were drawbacks. They had to be changed three to four times a day, since they got dull after a few hours' work. They had to have a large diameter to cut big logs, so they were thick, and they made a wide cut in the wood, or "cut a wide kerf," as sawyers say. That wasted lumber. Many New England sawyers, Mainers in particular, were skeptical of the new "buzz saw." Although it was used for edging, trimming, and cross-cutting, the circular saw was not in common use in Maine until about 1850.

The combination of steam power and the circular saw made portable sawmills possible. They could be set up and used all winter, then dismantled before mud season. Used in Maine before the 1880s, they were used to cut lumber for boxes, matchsticks, and other small products where there wasn't enough marketable timber to set up big logging operations. Good for harvesting "blow-downs" from windstorms, they tended to leave a mess in the woods—huge piles of slabs and sawdust. Combined with logging railroads, portable steam-powered sawmills enabled lumber companies to cut deeper into the forest.

The band saw was introduced in 1889. It was a continuous blade that ran around two huge wheels. By 1900 large sawmills were using them because they handled larger and heavier logs than circular saws. Band saws were expensive, but they were fast, cut a narrow kerf, and did not jam or heat up like circular saws.

Band saw wheels ran at a phenomenal speed of 3,000 feet (915 meters) per minute. To sharpen the band saw, men had to

stop the wheel, slip off the old saw, and put on a sharp one. They sharpened it twice a day. A log carriage went back and forth with two men riding on it, a dogger and a setter. The dogger pinned a log to the carriage with grab hooks. At a signal from the sawyer, the setter moved the log to cut the correct thickness. After each cut down the length of the log, the carriage jolted back for the log to be rotated by a mechanical log turner, an arm with ratchetlike teeth in it that shot up through the floor of the log deck. The log turner was one of the greatest sawmill inventions in years. After four cuts, the log was a squared-off timber, called a cant. The cant was then resawed into boards on a band or gang resaw.

Long logs are piled high, ready to be sawed into lumber at this steam-powered mill.

Close cooperation between the sawyer, the block setter, and the carriage riders was absolutely critical. Because sawmills are so noisy, it is impossible to be heard, so hand signal codes were devised. To turn the log for the next cut, for instance, the sawyer would raise his hand with his palm open, facing out. As soon as the carriage riders saw it, he would drop his hand to his side.

The sawyer was the most skilled man in the sawmill. He had to quickly size up each log. After cutting the first slab, he could tell more about its quality and signal messages to the setter.

Sawmills were, and still are, dangerous places. Among the most frequent accidents were drownings in millponds, while rolling logs onto lifts to go into the sawmill. Other casualties were falling onto a circular saw, getting tangled in the log turner chain, or being struck by a board or loose piece of wood thrown by a saw.

Saws broke. If a saw hit metal, it could throw wood through the roof, kill people, and damage saws. Sometimes metal spikes or nails were imbedded in a log. Loggers cut sugar maples four or five feet off the ground, to avoid sugaring-off nails. There were no safety guards on saws for many years. Most sawyers lost at least one finger to a saw. Men occasionally had their arms or legs cut off. It was easy for a man's sleeve to get caught in a saw, then the saw would grab his arm and cut it off.

Fires were a constant danger. Sawmills were highly susceptible to fire, particularly steam-powered mills. Their smokestacks spewed out sparks and men were continuously putting out fires. Sawmill fires were so common that in the nineteenth century, practically every sawmill in this country burned at least once.

To ward against fires, workers, sometimes children, swept up the sawdust. Plenty of water buckets were kept within easy reach in the mill and around the lumber yard and storage sheds. No smoking was allowed in a sawmill. Workers in one large mill in the Bangor area pumped water all over the outside of their building whenever sawing was going on. Another mill installed an automatic sprinkler system in 1889. The year 1945 brought the first legislation requiring spark arresters on sawmills. They were devices put on top of smokestacks to keep sparks from escaping and starting fires.

Floods posed a danger to sawmills, too, because most were built on riverbanks. In 1846 a flood on the Kennebec River swept fifty to sixty saws away. Entire sawmills were swept downstream in Bangor that same spring, along with bridges and houses.

Every colonial village in New England had a sawmill. It provided early families wood for their dwellings. Today, sawmills cut wood for our dwellings. Band saws are still used as headsaws, gang saws still cut big logs into thin boards all at once, and circular saws are used for edging and crosscutting lumber. And sawmills will still cut and trim lumber for years to come.

A SAWYER

CLUNK! The log drops onto the carriage, dripping wet from the millpond.

The high-pitched shriek of the enormous band saw goes through your whole body. WHEEEEEE!

Harvey and Slim ride the carriage. Harvey moves two levers that work "dogs" to clamp the log in place. Slim sets the thickness for each cut. You watch for their signals. When they nod "ready," you pull the carriage lever. WHOOSHHH! The first slab is cut.

You keep a constant eye on the log, watching for knots or other defects. After one slab is sawed off, Harvey flips the log turner and clamps the log again. Slim adjusts the thickness, and you make another slice. After four cuts, the timber is square, and it goes to the resaw.

Log after log, you saw away. "Where the devil did all these bumpy, twisting logs come from?" you grumble to no one in particular. No one could hear you anyway, with the horrendous noise in here. After a while, you draw your hand across your throat as if to slit it. "BREAK."

"Jerking back and forth on that carriage gets a guy all jittery," says Harvey, climbing down. "Good thing we need to change the blade, so we can get off every once in a while."

"It's the constant screaming of that saw that drives me berserk," adds Slim.

Harvey and Slim remove the dull band saw from the huge wheels, then take the sharp one off the grinding machine.

"Had a tiny crack in 'er," the filer says. "But I got 'er all welded up, so she won't explode on ya. Hammered and tensioned 'bout perfect, too."

You reset the sharp saw and start it up again. The whole place gets to vibrating as the huge band saw whirs up to speed.

You're about eight hours into your ten-hour day. You don't even see it! In a flash, the saw hits a spike in the log, and TWANG! The band snaps. Thirty feet of sharp steel ribbon snakes and swirls all about the mill.

Then you hear a bloodcurdling scream. "AACCC-CHHHH!"

Slim was in the way of the coiling beast. You stop the carriage and race to him.

You and Harvey lift Slim into the wagon, pressing his shoulder, so he won't bleed too badly. The teamster races you to town. If you get to the doctor soon, Slim should be okay. That blasted saw blade could have killed any one of you.

A chore boy sweeps sawdust away. He knows you don't want sparks catching the mill on fire.

Logging railroads penetrated the mountainous areas of New Hampshire by 1900. Long trestles were built to bridge streams and gorges.

Chapter 7

FULL STEAM AHEAD!

Over a knoll comes a monster—the most dramatic creation of iron that ever invaded the woods.

Walter M. MacDougall
"Lombard's Iron Monster,"
Yankee, March 1965

During the first half of the nineteenth century, most of America was becoming industrialized. Not in the woods. Men and horses remained the logging industry's "machines." Yet, by the end of World War I, a number of significant developments occurred that changed logging forever—and profoundly impacted the New England forest.

New technology came in the 1830s and 1840s, starting with steam engines. Early railroad locomotives burned almost 20,000 cords of wood a day and railroad tracks required millions of wooden ties each year. Many thousands of trees were cut for telegraph poles. Fortunately, about that time coal began to replace wood for fuel.

A major westward migration occurred in the 1850s. Most of New England's white pine had been cut, so loggers shifted to cutting spruce. Some of Maine's crackerjack lumbermen preferred to cut pine. They headed for New York and Pennsylvania, then on to forests in Michigan and Wisconsin, taking their methods with them. A few years later, when lumbering expanded rapidly out west, they moved all the way to the Pacific coast.

By the late 1890s logging railroads had invaded the forest. They could reach timber that had been too far from drivable streams to reach before, and they could haul hardwoods, which would not float, out to sawmills. Mountainous areas of New Hampshire that were too steep to log using horses now became accessible to the logging industry. More trees came down.

Tremendous changes occurred in the north woods when it became feasible to process wood fiber to make paper. Near the turn of the century, paper corporations bought millions of acres of forestland in northern Maine and New Hampshire and built giant pulp and paper mills. Within a few years, a few huge paper companies controlled Maine's major river systems and dominated its forest.

Paper companies built dirt roads into the woods. Trucks toted supplies into logging camps. The woods began to open up to the public. As automobiles became common, tourists drove north to enjoy New England's lakes and woods. Maine's Automobile Association even offered a self-guided "Pine Tree Tour" in 1914.

With all these changes, men and horses still moved the timber. On the verge of the twentieth century, a dramatic machine invaded the woods—the steam-driven log hauler. In 1899 the owner of a lumber company told inventor Alvin O. Lombard of Waterville, Maine, he hated ruining horses in the woods. Could Lombard come up with some mechanical way to haul logs? the gentleman wondered. Lombard figured he could easily use a steam engine for power. The problem he faced was getting traction on snow. If lags with teeth could revolve on rollers, a vehicle could crawl over rough roads through the woods. It was amazing! It was, in fact, the first practical application of a crawler-tread vehicle and the forerunner of military tanks and bulldozers.

As early as 1914, the Maine Automobile Association printed guidebooks so motorists could experience the beauty of the Maine woods.

In the early 1900s, steam log haulers, loaded with sleds of long logs, chugged through the woods of Maine and New Hampshire. It took four men to run this "iron monster"—a conductor, an engineer, a fireman, and a steersman.

Lombard received a patent for his tractor tread on May 21, 1901. His log hauler looked like a steam locomotive, except instead of wheels it had revolving belts of lags, and sled runners in front. The first models were fired by wood, then coal. The monsters traveled 4 to 6 miles (6 to 10 kilometers) per hour, weighed 10 to 30 tons each, and could haul as much lumber as sixteen horses. Later models could haul more. Headlamps were attached, so they could run day and night. They hauled heavy loads up slight inclines, which horses could not do.

Within ten years, Lombard's company was producing gasoline-driven log haulers. Without the huge steam boiler, the new model was smaller. It did not have the power of the steam engine, but it was more maneuverable and cost less to operate. Only one person was needed to run it. Best of all, it had brakes. Lombard phased out his steam haulers. Competition developed. By 1936 cheaper lag tractors were taking over the market. In thirty-five years, Lombard manufactured a total of eighty-three log haulers.

Steam log haulers required fairly level hauling roads because they had no brakes, and they did not operate well on more than a 2 percent incline. Hauling roads averaged 6 to 14 miles (10 to 23 kilometers) in length. Patrolmen were stationed along the route to keep roads clear and grooves well iced. Lumber was hauled on sleds, similar to the horse-drawn "two-sleds," but they were larger and much heavier. The longest "Lombard" trains had twenty-four sleds, more than 1/4-mile long, but most were less than ten sleds long. They reached up to 20 miles (32 kilometers) per hour going downhill. The train had to stop every 2 to 3 miles (3 to 5 kilometers) to take on fuel.

A steam log hauler required a four-man crew: a conductor, an engineer, a fireman, and a steersman.

The conductor was in charge of the train, so he directed loading and unloading at yards and landings. He made sure sleds were safely connected and logs chained securely onto them before moving the train. The conductor rode at the rear of the train, and he pulled a bell cord to signal the engineer in the cab. If his sled jumped the track going around a curve, he leaped off.

The engineer worked the throttle from the rear cab, but the only way he could control the speed was to throw the engine into reverse. He watched steam and water gauges carefully and had to fix breakdowns frequently.

A fireman threw slabs of wood (coal in some models) into the firebox to keep up the steam pressure.

The steersman sat up front and turned the runners with an iron steering wheel. There was no windshield, and in the early models, there was no roof over his head. Often, sparks from the smokestack burned holes in his clothes. Because the log hauler had no brakes, it occasionally got out of control. The steersman had a terrifying downhill ride!

Lombard's giant machines hauled logs from yards directly to rivers or sawmills. The steam log hauler allowed lumbermen to cut logs in one watershed and haul them to a different river. There was plenty of manual labor, however. Sleds had to be loaded and unloaded by hand, needing fifteen to twenty cant dog men each time.

Lombard's mammoth machine was familiar in the Maine and New Hampshire woods, and a few other places, for the first three decades of the twentieth century. Although its history was brief, the cumbersome iron monster holds an important place in the advancement of logging. For the first time, a machine did the work of horses in the woods.

A LOG HAULER STEERSMAN

Here you sit up front in the steering box again, open to the wind. You wrap your coat collar as high as you can around your face and neck. The train of empty sleds bounces along behind you as you steer *Nina* into the woods. The cold is so fierce, you can barely grip the wheel. Smoke in your face makes you cough and choke. For weeks now, you have been hauling logs out of the woods, about 10 miles. The crew has been making two runs a day to get all the winter's cut to the sawmill before spring. You have to use the headlamp for the second run, which will last until well after dark.

The engineer stops to refuel. He and the fireman load slabs of wood from the pile beside the hauling road. You finally arrive at the yard, where cant dog men load the sleds. When the logs are all chained on to each sled bunk, the conductor waves to the engineer, climbs atop a sled at the rear of the long train, and you're off.

Nina is chugging away, blowing steam and smoke all over the place. The confounded sparks keep burning holes in your clothes.

You are out front all alone. If something goes wrong way back, the conductor will pull the bell cord and the engineer will throw the log hauler into reverse.

This next turn is the worst. *Nina* is belching so much smoke, you cannot see where you are going. She always picks up speed heading around this curve. You hope you can keep her in the sled tracks. Oh, no! She's slipping! She's getting away from you! You come around the curve, turning the wheel as hard as you can. Dag nab it! The deer have eaten the hay off the hill again. You can't slow down! *Nina* has no brakes. You cling on and steer for your life! You're going faster and faster—up to 20 miles an hour! The train is fishtailing like crazy.

CRASH! The whole load jackknifes, and suddenly you are plopped into a 10-foot snowbank. Some of the sleds break loose and end up in the other snowbank. Chains break, and tons of loose logs scatter every which way—rolling all over the icy road.

The conductor jumps off in time. "Gallopin' gobbie birds!" he yells. "What a mess!"

The blacksmith will have a horrid job repairing all this. And the cant dog men will be swearing to have to reload all those logs.

Chapter 8

FIRE! AND OTHER DISASTERS!

Of all the foes which attack the woodlands of North America no other is so terrible as fire.

Gifford Pinchot, Forester
A Primer of Forestry,
Part I, 1903

Forest fires are as old as the forest. They can quickly devastate thousands of acres of trees. It takes almost one hundred years to fully recover from a severe fire.

Everyone fears fire. Yet until the twentieth century, we paid little attention to the fact that lightning was not the only cause of forest fires. We were causing them, too. Piles of dried-up branches littered the forest floor, left there by loggers. That debris, called slash, created a serious fire hazard. Sparks from logging railroad locomotives started fires. So did careless sportsmen and campers.

Forest fires started by carelessness have been cut drastically since Smokey Bear appeared in 1945. The U.S. Forest Service created him to tell all Americans: "Only you can prevent forest fires."

Back in 1891 the Maine State Forest Commission was created. New Maine laws required railroads to clear areas along tracks and install spark arresters on their smokestacks. Later, diesel locomotives further reduced fire hazards.

In the early 1900s the new Maine Forestry District started fire control programs, provided forest rangers, fire wardens, and fire-fighting equipment. Congress passed a law which provided federal funds for states to fight forest fires.

Logging operations left thousands of acres of slash in the woods, which was one cause of forest fires.

There were once more than one hundred active fire towers in Maine. Only three still operate, all staffed by volunteers. This tower at Ossipee Hill in Waterboro replaces the one destroyed during devastating forest fires in 1947.

From 1905 to 1991, lookout towers were a major fire control method in Maine. On June 10, 1905, the first continuously operated tower in the United States opened on top of Big Squaw Mountain (now called Big Moose Mountain), near Moosehead Lake. Fire towers were wooden at first, then replaced with steel structures. In all, more than one hundred fire towers were built in Maine. They had to be tied down with steel cables to withstand severe winds, ice, and snow. Lightning damage was a constant threat and towers received many direct hits.

Early fire tower watchmen backpacked supplies up remote mountain trails. There they made camp for the summer. Some nailed saw blades across their cabin windows to keep out bears! Most were men, but women also served.

A telephone system with almost 2,000 miles (3,220 kilometers) of phone lines was installed across northern Maine. It was extremely effective in forest fire control, and was used for emergency calls and search-and-rescue operations as well.

At first, lookout towers had no maps, but soon a circular map with degree markings around the rim became common. Horizon sketches were drawn and identified around the map's outer edge. The center of the map was the exact spot where that particular tower was located. An alidade was a sighting device that swiveled around that center. By pointing it at a fire, the azimuth (degrees from north) could be read. This told the direction of the fire. If another tower could also see the fire, the two azimuth readings pinpointed the fire's precise location.

Disastrous forest fires in 1947 burned more than 200,000 acres (81,000 hectares) of Maine. In York County, the fire came up over the top of Ossipee Hill, forcing the lookout watchman to abandon the fire tower. Soon after that, New England and New York coordinated fire prevention efforts. Later, Quebec and New Brunswick joined.

The state began closing towers in the 1960s, when it became cheaper to hire pilots for aerial fire spotting. Maine closed all towers in 1991, but three in southern Maine remain active through a volunteer program. New Hampshire still operates about fifteen fire towers.

Surface fires are rarely hot enough to destroy large trees, but their bark is damaged, and seedlings and saplings are destroyed. Ground fires burn underneath the forest floor and carry fire underground. Crown fires are so hot, they bake tree oils into the soil, so it cannot absorb water for a long time. Dry pine trees literally explode, scattering sparks long distances.

Fighting a forest fire often means confining it and letting it burn itself out. Maine has many natural barriers, such as ponds and lakes and wide rivers. Depending on the size of the fire and wind velocity, a wider barrier may be "burned out" to remove fuel ahead of a fire. And a firefighter's primary goal is to remove dry brush from the fire's path. Wind can speed fire through the forest, or put it out by turning it back over its burned-out path. In other parts of the United States, planes drop fire retardants, but in Maine there is enough water supply, so chemical retardants are not needed to fight fire. Water is dropped from helicopters. Sometimes, however,

This forest fire is burning along the ground. Surface fires destroy young forest growth and damage the bark of large trees. They also disrupt habitats of forest-dwelling animals.

firefighters mix a soaplike foam with water to help it soak into the ground and wet the area.

Hand tools are still the primary fire-fighting equipment—axes, shovels, rakes, and grub hoes. In the 1920s a portable pump made it possible to carry water to fire lines. Power pumps and chain saws became available after World War II, along with portable field telephones and ground-to-aircraft communication. Today, aerial spotting is effective, with use of global positioning systems. While planes are important, firefighters in Maine do not parachute from them, as they do elsewhere. Most parts of Maine, even in the deep wilderness, are accessible to vehicles, thanks to paper companies' logging roads. With enough time, bulldozers can reach most areas to cut a wide fire barrier. Fire crews can be flown in by helicopter if necessary.

The climate of the northern New England forest tends to be humid, the ground often moist. Therefore, forest fires are not as common as they are in western and southern states. Yet droughts do occur and precautions are taken to prevent fires. Maine state forest rangers maintain fire equipment, keeping tools on their trucks at all times, ready to use.

Fire is not the forest's only natural enemy. Floods, avalanches, and wind can also kill quickly. In 1938 a hurricane blew down millions of trees in New England. In the White Mountain National Forest alone, the flattened trees would have built almost 11,000 homes.

Insects and diseases cause more damage than the rapid killers. Only a handful of insects are destructive, such as the gypsy moth

Fire prevention and control are important parts of a forest ranger's job. Rangers keep fire-fighting equipment on their trucks, ready to use at any time—tools such as hoses, pumps, grub hoes, and shovels.

A firefighter keeps close watch over a forest fire. Sometimes, to keep a fire from spreading, crews clear out a strip ahead of it, removing burnable forest matter.

and white pine blister rust, both of which were accidentally imported. Spruce budworm kills firs as well as spruce. Large spruce-fir forests, such as are found in northern Maine, suffer from periodic outbreaks. Forest fires often start in budworm-killed stands. In a sort of vicious cycle, disease and insects tend to attack trees already damaged by fire, then spread to nearby healthy ones.

Foresters have learned that too much fire fighting is as bad as none. Fire does clear out debris and release nutrients that help keep the forest vigorous. Small fires remove dead trees and brush and help prevent devastating crown fires. Prescribed burns are an essential fire management tool on federal lands, primarily in western states. They are occasionally used in the White Mountain and Green Mountain national forests of New England. Carefully watched, the fires must be hot enough to burn the surface duff so seeds can grow, but not so hot they kill mature trees.

Forest fires are violent and destructive. Nature is persistent, however, and forests do regenerate after disasters. Recovery is slow by human terms, but sure.

A FIRE TOWER WATCH

Your two-way radio spits static, but you get the message. "ATTENTION: U.S. Weather Bureau Reporting: Fire danger for today, October 15. Very High, Level Four. Repeat: Very High."

You have been in this tower ten hours every day since the first of May. Fire danger has been high for weeks. In dry times like this, it is critical to keep a constant watch for new smokes. You keep looking through your binoculars in every direction. Black smoke means a structure fire. If the smoke is grayish or white, it's a forest fire.

Off to the southeast, you spot something. You take a sighting on the alidade on your round map table. The rim of the map shows a drawing of the mountains, to help you pinpoint fires.

You are glad you finished fixing that phone line, after the moose got tangled in it the other day. When you hike down for supplies, you'll have to lug some more wire up the mountain.

"Frank? Tower 31 calling—11:15 A.M. I am spotting a small fire at azimuth 125°, about 10 miles from here. It is likely Camp Pretty Pines."

"I wish campers would be more careful to extinguish their campfires," says Frank. "I'll send a ranger over."

While you enter the report details into the tower notebook, you notice your new poster hanging above the desk. "Hey, Smokey," you say to it. "We'll help people learn to prevent forest fires!" The Forest Service created Smokey Bear a year or so ago, about the end of World War II. In a few months you will take posters with you to introduce Smokey Bear to students.

By afternoon, haze is interfering with your visibility, but you see something in the direction of Tower 35. Is it haze or white smoke? you wonder. You plot the location on your map.

"Hello, Frank? Tower 31 calling again. I have a smoke at azimuth 265°, near where lightning struck two days ago. Could have been smoldering. Can Tower 35 see anything?"

"I will call her right away," says Frank.

A moment later Frank is back on the line. "She did get a read. The warden is on his way."

In a few years they'll have airplanes surveying this entire state, you figure. Pilots would be able to spot fires from way off.

In the notebook, you record, "2:30 P.M. Spotted smoke at azimuth 265°, 15 to 20 miles away. Wind southwest 8 to 10 miles per hour. Lightning fire beginning to smoke up."

Frank calls again. "Better stay in your tower tonight to relay messages. This could be a big one if the wind picks up."

Chapter 9

MANAGING OUR FORESTS TODAY

When I was eight years old, I fell in love with the forest and I decided then that I wanted to be a forester when I grew up. I am fortunate that this chosen career in forestry has enabled me to travel throughout the world teaching about and conducting research on the forest resources that I love.

G. Bruce Wiersma
*Professor of Forest Resources and
Dean of the College of Natural
Sciences, Forestry, and Agriculture
University of Maine,
Orono, Maine, 2001*

Gone are the old-time loggers and river drivers. Gone are the oxen and horses and log haulers. World War II brought significant advances in tree harvesting equipment. Chain saws and other power equipment replaced earlier logging methods. Developments continued. Today, trees are harvested by huge machines—feller-bunchers, skidders, and cut-to-length harvesters. Trucks rumble down the roads with long logs, some headed for sawmills, others for chipping plants to be ground into pulp or as biomass fuel.

Woodsmen have cut the northern woods for more than 350 years, but until the twentieth century, no one managed them. The word forestry was not even in dictionaries until 1860. It means the science of developing or caring for forests.

Modern forestry began in this country in 1898, with President McKinley's appointment of Gifford Pinchot as chief of the federal Forestry Division. Pinchot initiated programs for forest reserves. Theodore Roosevelt created the United States Forest Service in 1905, and named Pinchot its first chief forester. New England and three Middle Atlantic States form its northeastern region.

Logging has played a significant part in northern New England's culture and economy since early colonial days. Maine has a particularly strong interest in the forest, for its forest is immense. Maine has about 17.5 million acres (7 million hectares) of forest, almost 90 percent of the state. No other state in the country has such a large percentage of forest. Maine's forest is larger than the entire states of New Hampshire, Vermont, and Massachusetts combined.

Maine's first forest commissioner was appointed in 1891. In 1900 the University of Maine offered a course in forestry. Three years later its Department of Forestry offered a full undergraduate degree program, one of four in the United States at that time. The Maine Forestry District was formed in 1909, lasting until 1972, when it became the Maine Forest Service.

The Weeks Law, enacted in 1911, authorized the federal government to buy privately owned timberlands to establish national forests. That paved the way for the White Mountain National Forest in New Hampshire (including a tiny fraction of western Maine) and the Green Mountain National Forest in Vermont. Under the Weeks Law, timber could still be harvested, but only under the supervision of trained foresters.

In the early 1900s companies began hiring industrial foresters. They were not welcome at first. Forestry management, or silviculture, is the science of managing forest resources to produce timber and ensure future timber yield, while protecting water and wildlife, and preserving recreational areas. Techniques are tailored to individual forests.

Management is not easy, for the forest is complex and constantly changing. Forest ecosystems process water. They absorb rainfall and release stored water through streams and springs, removing pollutants from groundwater. Trees help reduce the rate of carbon

Students conduct research in many aspects of forestry, such as soil chemistry, forest ecology, and tree diseases. More and more, they are becoming involved in public education.

dioxide buildup in the atmosphere. They also cool us. Soil, water, and wildlife are part of the ecosystem, too. Disturbances, such as disease, insect infestation, fire, and wind, are normal.

Men and women are trained in college to be foresters. They learn the details of forest life and how to apply that knowledge to managing forests. They may work independently, for state or national agencies, or for companies. Foresters plan and oversee tree harvesting and replanting, and they deal with forest disturbances. Increasingly, foresters are learning to deal with people's concerns about the environment.

Foresters learn that to preserve a forest means to leave natural conditions as they are, letting them change on their own. Forest conservation, on the other hand, is managing forests for timber, water, wildlife, and recreation. It means overseeing natural resources to be sure of adequate present and future needs. Most foresters consider a managed forest healthier than wild woods, for the trees are more vigorous and disease resistant. More and more, conservation includes recreational use of the woods and people's sense of beauty.

Many northern foresters today follow a system of preserving some unique areas of forest, intensively managing about 10 to 12 percent (which often means clear-cutting to plant desired species), and harvesting most of the forest at a slower, natural rate. One-half cord per acre is about the yearly rate of growth for mixed soft-wood and hardwood stands in the northern forest.

Most corporations who own woodlands in Maine manage them according to certification standards. Harvesting and replanting standards are improving each year, with more and more landown-ers participating. Millions of acres of Maine forest are already under some certification.

Foresters learn a variety of harvesting methods. Seed tree cut-ting is removing all except a few trees for reseeding. Shelterwood cutting is a series of cuttings extended over several years. Big trees protect small ones until small ones grow up. Selective cutting is cutting some large, mature trees, repeatedly every ten to fifteen years. This method thins a stand, encouraging growth of younger trees and new reproduction.

After trees are cut and piled, a huge skidder hauls them away to a truck or railroad siding. In early logging operations, horses and teamsters did the hauling, or skidding, as shown on page 38.

Clear-cutting leaves open acreage and can be seeded immediately. Like a forest fire or a hurricane, clear-cutting is a major forest disturbance. It takes decades to recover from clear-cuts. They interrupt the food chain, wildlife cycles, and vegetation. Only what can adapt will survive. Migration corridors and heat absorption of land and water are also affected. And, of course, natural beauty is destroyed. Yet many wildlife scientists and foresters (including the Maine Forest Service) accept clear-cutting as a viable forestry tool—within limits. Most often, a single clear-cut today is less than 10 acres (4 hectares), and rarely is it necessary to clear-cut more than 100 acres (41 hectares). One reason for clear-cutting is spruce budworm, which kills spruce and fir trees.

Spruce budworm is a difficult part of the northern forest's cycle. Millions of acres of Maine are covered with spruce and fir trees. One outbreak of spruce budworm lasted from 1909 to 1918. It killed 70 percent of Maine's spruce/fir forest. Old stands are the worst affected and become a fire danger, so foresters prefer mixed-age stands, with young and old trees in the same area. Both clear-cutting and partial cutting are recommended treatment. Large-scale clear-cutting took place due to a spruce budworm infestation in the 1970s. A public outcry by environmentalists resulted in the 1989 Maine Forest Practices Act, which aims to restrict and regulate clear-cutting.

That was not the first public outcry. In the 1950s and 1960s, environmentalists raised public awareness and concern about a number of issues affecting us all. DDT, successful in reducing insects and diseases, was found to produce severe environmental effects, so it was banned. Polluted rivers forced a Maine law that ended log driving and led to laws against dumping toxic waste. When it was learned that smokestacks in the Midwest were causing acid precipitation over New England, people began fighting against pollution.

Protection of endangered species became important. Plants and animals gained value regardless of their usefulness to humans. The public began to place higher value on forests as an aesthetic background than as a source of useful products. Concern grew about proper management of forests, wilderness areas, and public water supply watersheds.

We know a lot more about managing forests than we did a century ago. Still, forestry research continues. The University of Maine conducts research in cooperation with specialists in many fields of environmental science and forest resources: soils, climatic conditions, air pollutants, diseases of trees, wetlands, water quality, fish and wildlife, interdependence of ecosystems, effects of fire, and much more—even the impact of recreational vehicles on the forest ecosystem. Other places conduct research, too.

Forest management involves much more than trees. It involves listening to public interests and concerns as well. There is much to learn.

These forestry students are studying a satellite map of Maine, focusing on forested areas and watersheds.

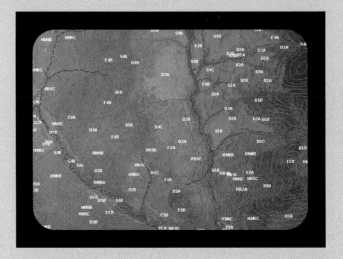

A Day in the Life of...

A FORESTER

The map on the computer shows details of the company's woodlands. "This stand is heavy to softwood," says Tim, pointing to one site on the screen. Together you read the site detail code—species, height, density of the stand, and average tree size. "We may need to cut in this plot in the next year or two. Store it on your handheld computer, and take notes when you cruise the site today."

In forestry school you studied wood science, botany, forest engineering, and ecosystems. You researched soils, diseases of trees, and acid precipitation. Some of your college classmates will work in forestry research and education, others for federal or state governments, and some will be independent foresters. You are starting a job as a corporate forester. You and your co-workers will recommend forest management techniques, based on details, such as tree species, moisture, soil content, and wildlife habitats.

Tim explains that you will spend three to four days a week in the woods, all year long. The rest will be at your desk making planting and harvesting plans and writing reports.

"Lots of paperwork," adds Catherine with a smile, "and meetings to attend."

On the drive to the woodlands, Catherine stops to observe a harvesting operation. "Grab your hard hat," she says, parking the truck. "I want to talk with Roger."

Roger is operating a feller-buncher. You watch its arm reach out, cut one tree, then two more—all in a few seconds. Roger swings the arm around, tips it, and drops the bunch of trees onto the pile.

Roger stops the machine and steps out of his cab. "Can you believe my great-grandfather was a logger, too?" he says. "He cut trees with a crosscut saw and hauled logs with horses. Here I sit in an air-conditioned cab. It doesn't select which trees to cut, though," he adds, chuckling.

"Tim and Catherine paint their trees for me. Not all foresters do. On some jobs I have to decide myself." You watch the skidder haul the long logs to a portable saw, where they are cut into 12- to 16-foot sawlogs. Some of these trees are not lumber quality, so Roger piles those to be put through the chipper.

Back in the truck, Catherine explains, "Environmental issues are hot topics these days. State law restricts tree harvesting. We have to file harvesting intentions for every job. State foresters try to make sure we obey the rules." She further explains how you will work out projections on the computer and report to Tim.

"Grab your hard hat again, plus your handheld computer," says Catherine, "and don't forget your compass."

"Why do we need a compass with a GPS [global positioning system] on this computer?" you ask.

"Rule number one. Always carry your compass—in case something goes wrong with your instruments. It is easy to lose your bearings in the woods." She clicks the truck's location into her computer. "There. It's stored in memory, so at day's end, we can find it easily."

You walk through the forest, examining trees, water, soil, and wildlife habitats. On your handheld computer, you log into the site. Here is the road layout and the stream you saw back in Tim's office. You add this storm-flow culvert to the data.

After you eat your picnic lunch, you hike to the site the company clear-cut a few months ago. You groan. "This looks like a war zone."

"It is a mess," Catherine admits, "but it will heal. We'll plant seedlings here in the fall. You will be supervising planting, too, as part of your job. Tomorrow," she continues, "I'm bringing a school group here for a woods tour. They'll be horrified, too. They always groan. Then we bus to a site that was clear-cut ten to twelve years ago, and they're amazed it looks like a forest already."

"This trailing arbutus is a protected plant, isn't it?" you ask, as you pass a sandy bank along the dirt road. Catherine nods. "So is this lady's slipper," she adds, pointing at another spot. "Mark them in your computer. We record protected plants in our reports."

Quietly, you walk through the woods, noting details. You hear something rustling in the underbrush across a little bog. For a moment you watch a doe with her fawn, then walk on.

Chapter 10

THE FOREST OR THE TREES—OR BOTH?

Perhaps the ideal state is to have forests of all ages, young, medium, and old in the landscape. This will provide the highest diversity of habitats and therefore the opportunity for the largest number of species to live in that landscape.

Dr. Patrick Moore
Greenspirit Consultancy,
Vancouver, BC, 2000
Former member and founder
of Greenpeace

More than three hundred years have come and gone since British monarchs imposed the Broad Arrow Policy on New England colonists. Today, different concerns surround the northern forest, no less controversial.

Forests, like all living things, continually change. Trees do not live forever, whether we cut them or not. Should we let trees rot? Or should we cut them, use the wood, and plant new trees? Opinions vary from one extreme to the other—from not allowing any tree harvesting to letting landowners do all the harvesting they want to on their own land. In all likelihood, the best answers lie somewhere in between.

The forest is vital to New England's economy. Thousands of jobs, such as logging and papermaking, depend directly on being able to harvest trees. Yet tourism is an important source of income, and much of that depends on *not* harvesting too many trees. Vacationers travel to the north woods from all over the world to enjoy the scenery. They camp and hike along wilderness trails, fish and boat on the many lakes and rivers, ski and snowboard on the mountain slopes, and cruise the woodlands on off-road vehicles.

Indeed, most of us enjoy the woods. We also enjoy the benefits we derive from wood products. We like living in wood homes, and some of us heat those homes with wood fuel. Our rooms are filled with wooden furniture. We use tons and tons of paper. And on a summer afternoon, we like to whack a base hit with a wooden baseball bat! You can make a sizable list of the wood products you use in a single day.

The United States uses more raw material per person than any other country on Earth. Wood is a renewable resource. Fossil fuels are not. And every substitute for wood products takes more energy to produce—plastic, steel, and aluminum. On the other hand, we must not chop away at our forests needlessly. Surely we can do a better job of conserving our use of paper and other wood products.

Scientists are continually researching more effective ways to ensure a healthy forest environment and to fight tree diseases and other disturbances the future may bring. There will be more advances in technology and wood science, such as genetically engineered tree seedlings.

No doubt, we have mistreated the forest in the past. Early logging methods wasted timber. We carelessly started forest fires and we clear-cut large tracts of forestland. Some still abuse forest resources, despite regulations.

We need to consider several forest issues. The public wants to retain access to the forest for recreation and to experience its beauty. Some people feel that a larger portion of the forest should be preserved as wilderness, and that additional laws are the only way to protect it. Others fear that government control would end individual property rights. Off-road vehicles wreak havoc on the forest environment, yet every year more of them invade the woods. Some believe their use should be restricted. Debates will continue over regulations of our forest.

Clear-cutting is New England's ugliest forest issue. Not only do clear-cuts *look* ugly, they can spark ugly political battles. Should we ban clear-cutting? Should we further restrict it? Or are current regulations sufficient? Tremendous public concern surrounds this issue. Most citizens do not clearly understand the facts about clear-cutting, but nearly everyone has an opinion. Emotions run high. No one, it seems, is neutral about the forest. People will continue to argue over harvesting methods, or whether there should even be any harvesting at all.

More and more frequently, legislative proposals are being brought to the public. People are voting directly on issues that affect the future of the northern forest. These issues are *not* simple. We cannot believe all the political appeals we see and hear. We need to learn more about all sides of environmental issues if we are to make informed choices. We will continue to have to decide about forest issues as new concerns arise.

Billions of trees are growing in New England today. Some are as large as the king's mast pines of colonial days. Tiny seedlings no bigger than your little finger are growing, too. The forest is alive.

Difficult choices lie ahead. We need forests, yet we need forest products. It *is* possible to cut enough trees to meet our needs, and at the same time, protect enough trees and plant enough seedlings to replenish the forest. We *can* have wood, while we enjoy the benefits of a thriving forest. If we make responsible environmental decisions in the future, we can have our forests—and our trees!

LOGGING TIMELINE

1609	Explorer Henry Hudson cuts a ship's mast on the shore of Penobscot Bay.
1630s	One of the country's earliest sawmills is built in South Berwick, Maine.
1634	First supply of New England pine masts reaches England.
1691	William and Mary initiate the Broad Arrow Policy.
1761–1762	Forest fires in southern New Hampshire and Maine probably set by colonists to keep the king from getting masts.
1775	Colonists refuse to ship masts to England after Battle of Lexington and Concord.
1776	United States declares independence.
1797	U.S.S. *Constitution* launched. Masts made from Maine pines.
1820	Maine becomes a state.
1832	Maine's Bangor & Old Town Railroad is chartered, one of nation's earliest (12-mile [19-kilometer]-long rail line to carry lumber).
1830s	Bangor, Maine, is the world's busiest shipping port for lumber until the 1880s.
1858	Joseph Peavey invents peavey cant dog.
1860	Word forestry first appears in the dictionary.
1868	First river drive on upper Connecticut River. Twenty million feet (6,100,000 meters) of timber are driven from northern New Hampshire to Holyoke, Massachusetts.

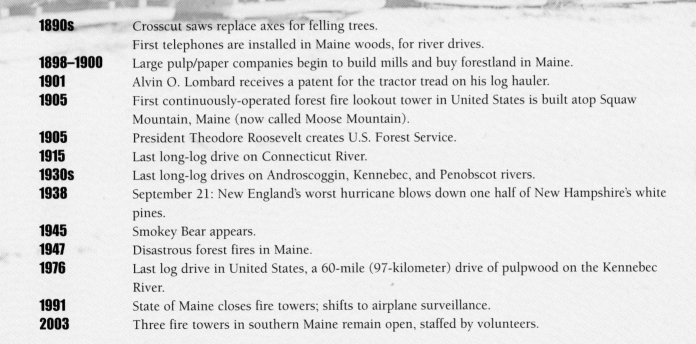

1890s	Crosscut saws replace axes for felling trees.
	First telephones are installed in Maine woods, for river drives.
1898–1900	Large pulp/paper companies begin to build mills and buy forestland in Maine.
1901	Alvin O. Lombard receives a patent for the tractor tread on his log hauler.
1905	First continuously-operated forest fire lookout tower in United States is built atop Squaw Mountain, Maine (now called Moose Mountain).
1905	President Theodore Roosevelt creates U.S. Forest Service.
1915	Last long-log drive on Connecticut River.
1930s	Last long-log drives on Androscoggin, Kennebec, and Penobscot rivers.
1938	September 21: New England's worst hurricane blows down one half of New Hampshire's white pines.
1945	Smokey Bear appears.
1947	Disastrous forest fires in Maine.
1976	Last log drive in United States, a 60-mile (97-kilometer) drive of pulpwood on the Kennebec River.
1991	State of Maine closes fire towers; shifts to airplane surveillance.
2003	Three fire towers in southern Maine remain open, staffed by volunteers.

GLOSSARY

acid precipitation: rain, sleet, or snow that has been polluted by acid chemicals

adze: tool with its blade set crosswise to the handle, used for hewing or shaving timber

alidade [**AL i dade**]: sighting device to locate the direction of a forest fire

axhead: the steel chopping head of an ax

azimuth [**AZ i muth**]: degrees from north. Two azimuth readings from different locations pinpoint the exact location of a forest fire.

band saw: continuous steel band with sawteeth on one or both edges, turning around two huge wheels

barrel staves: wood strips cut to make a barrel

bateau [**bah TOW**], **pl., bateaux** [**bah TOWS**]: a long boat, pointed at both ends, used by river crews on eastern log drives

bedding crew: crew that cut a bed of boughs and small evergreens where a large mast pine was to be felled, to soften the impact and prevent the mast pine from breaking

biomass [**BIO mass**]: shredded forest vegetation

blaze: to mark trees with a shallow ax cut

blowdown: a tree or area of forest that has been blown over by wind

board foot: unit of measure for lumber equal to the volume of a board 1 foot wide, 1 foot long, and 1 inch thick, or a total of 144 cubic inches

boom: logs chained together, end to end, to corral loose logs to be pulled, or a string of floating logs to guide loose logs past an obstruction

bowsprit: a long pole sticking out from the bow (front) of a ship to allow more sail area

bridle chain: a chain wrapped around a sled runner for a brake

Broad Arrow mark: mark used to reserve property for the British government. In the American colonies, large white pine trees were marked for masts and spars for the British Royal Navy.

Broad Arrow policy: Britain's policy of reserving large pine trees, and prohibiting colonists from cutting them for their own use. It was much resented by colonists, and one of the issues that sparked the Revolutionary War.

broadax: ax with a wide blade for hewing timber

buck: to cut a tree into shorter logs after felling

bullwhacker: an oxen driver

burn out: to burn a barrier ahead of a forest fire to stop its spread

butt: base of a tree trunk or large end of a log

calks [cocks]: steel spikes in the soles of river drivers' boots or on horseshoes. "Calked boots" allowed men to stand or walk on moving logs. "Calked shoes" had studs to keep horses from slipping on icy logging roads.

cant: a log that has been squared off in a sawmill, before being cut into boards

cant dog: a lumberman's basic tool, a pole with a hook (dog) and a spike at the end, used for rolling logs. The tool, commonly called a cant dog in Maine and New Hampshire, is called a peavey elsewhere. Cant dog men were crews who loaded sleds at landings and yards.

capstan: vertical post or spool, used to wind a rope or cable

carriage: a frame on which are mounted the mechanisms for holding a log while it is being sawed. It moves on tracks, back and forth past the saw.

chipper: machine that chips logs and bark into small pieces

chopper: a basic member of a logging crew who fells trees and makes them into logs; a woodchopper. (The term *lumberjack* originated farther west.)

circular saw: round saw for cutting across logs or lumber

clear-cutting: clearing all the trees in a forested area at one time

cookee [cook EE]: cook's helper in a logging camp

cord: unit of measure of stacked round wood, 4 feet x 4 feet x 8 feet

corduroy road: a road built of logs laid crosswise

crosscut saw: a large two-man saw, with handles on each end, for sawing trees or logs

crown fire: forest fire that reaches the tops of trees

cruise: to inspect a stand of timber in order to estimate yield by varieties, to lay out roads, and to select a spot for a camp. The person who does it is called a timber cruiser.

cut: in the woods, a season's output of logs

cut-to-length harvester: tree-harvesting machine, usually called CTL, that fells a tree, removes its limbs, and cuts it into desired lengths, according to a computerized order

DDT: insecticide sprayed on plants to rid them of insects or disease. Its use is no longer permitted.

deacon seat: the one classic piece of camp furniture, usually made of half a log, flat side up, with stick legs

dingle: open midsection of a type of logging camp, with the cooking area at one end and the bunkhouse at the other

dogger: sawmill worker who controls the device that secures the log on the carriage for sawing

duff: partly-decayed vegetation on the forest floor

feller-buncher: tree-harvesting machine, which grasps standing trees, cuts through their trunks, and lays them down. The operator sits in an enclosed cab.

felling: New England term for cutting trees

fetlocks: the tufted areas on the backs of horses' legs, just above the hooves

freshet: runoff, or sudden flooding of a stream. Spring freshets helped carry logs downstream.

gang saw: a parallel row of saw blades in one frame for sawing lumber into several boards at once

goad: hickory rod with a sharp steel point on one end for prodding oxen

GPS: acronym for Global Positioning System

grindstone: a large stone disk that spins on a shaft when pedaled, used for sharpening axes

grub hoe: hand tool to gouge out dirt, roots, or rocks, used by firefighters to keep small fires from spreading

haul: on a log jam, to let loose quickly

headsaw: the primary log-cutting saw in a sawmill

headworks: a raft with a capstan in the middle, operated by men or steam power, used to pull booms of logs across lakes and ponds

hew [hyoo]: to trim or shape a piece of timber with a broadax or adze

holding dam: large dam with gates to control water level on a river, pond, or lake

hovel [HAW vel]: primitive barn to house logging animals

inkslinger: nickname for a camp clerk

kerf: the space made by a saw as it cuts through timber

key log: a log, lodged or caught in the river, that caused a jam

kickback: action when the butt of a falling tree jumps backward over the stump instead of dropping forward

landing: place where logs were assembled for loading onto sleds or to be rolled into a river

limb: to remove the limbs from a felled tree

log drive: transporting a mass of logs from the woods downriver to a mill; also called a river drive, or simply a drive

logging: lumbering or harvesting of trees, a process which consists of felling trees, removing branches, sawing trees into smaller logs, and moving them out of the woods

logging operation: entire lumbering project, which includes cruising, construction of camp, hiring, feeding, bedding, chopping, hauling, and, in the old days, driving

log hauler: a crawler tractor used to pull many sleds of logs coupled together. The first models ran by steam, later by gasoline.

log turner: a toothed lever used to turn logs on a sawmill carriage. Its movements are controlled by the sawyer.

long johns: heavy wool long underwear, usually red

lumber: logs sawed into usable boards and planks

mackinaw [MAC in aw]: heavy wool jacket, usually plaid

mast: a long upright pole on a ship to hold sails and rigging

mast pine: native eastern white pine suitable for a ship's mast, smaller spars, and yardarms. In Maine, a tall, straight white pine is still sometimes called a mast pine.

peavey: wooden lever with a strong steel spike and a hook at the end, used for turning and rolling logs. Joseph Peavey, a Maine blacksmith, improved the original cant dog in 1858, by hinging the hook so it didn't flop laterally but always stayed in line with the shaft. His invention is often called a cant dog in Maine and New Hampshire.

pickpole or pike pole: a long pole with a spike, or steel point on one end, used to guide logs that are floating in lakes or rivers and to prod them through sorting booms

pulpwood: wood cut into 4-foot lengths, used in manufacturing paper

Québécois [Keh be QUAW]: people from Quebec, Canada

resaw: a mill saw that cuts lumber into smaller boards; also the process of sawing boards

river hog: a river driver

roll dam: a small dam that logs can roll over when the water is high enough

rule: measuring device marked to estimate the board footage in a log

sacking the rear: working the tail end of a log drive, rolling all stranded logs back into the mainstream

sawlogs: sections of trees, nearly always the trunks, that are sold to be cut into lumber. Sawlogs are distinguished from logs that will be chipped or otherwise processed for pulp, fuel, or manufactured products, such as particleboard or plywood.

saw pit: in colonial times, a pit dug for sawing logs lengthwise into timbers, using a two-man saw (pit saw). One man standing on or above the log, pulled the saw up, and the other, standing in a pit below, pulled it down.

scale: to measure the number of board feet in a log

seed tree cutting: tree harvesting process that cuts all but a few trees, left for reseeding

selective cutting: cutting a portion of the mature trees in a stand, usually those marked by a forester

setter: sawmill worker who guides the saw to cut a log the correct thickness

shelterwood cutting: system of tree harvesting that cuts an area in a series over several years, leaving some large trees to protect young ones

silviculture: forest management, intended to protect future timber yield, water, wildlife, and recreational areas

sinkers: doughnuts

skidder: machine that drags logs or tree lengths out of the woods

slash: branches, treetops, and debris left on the ground after logging

sled bunk: platform on a logging sled on which the logs were piled

sluiced: what happens when a team of horses hauling a load of logs gets out of control and goes off the road

sluiceway: chute built to channel logs down past a rough area, often beside a dam

snub line: heavy rope or cable attached to a loaded sled and wrapped around a tree at the top of a steep hill; used to ease the sled down the hill safely

snub machine: improved device for slowing a snub line

sorting boom: area where men direct logs into separate areas, guided by the marks (similar to cattle brands) on the logs

spar: pole (mast, yardarm, bowsprit) used for supporting sails on a ship

spark arresters: devices put on sawmill chimneys and railroad engine smokestacks to keep sparks from escaping

splash dam: temporary dam on a small tributary, built to hold water until time to let logs through to the main stream, then removed

sprinkler wagon: a large water tank on a sled, used to ice logging roads

spruce gum: sticky sap balls found on the outer bark of spruce trees, often chewed by woodsmen

stamping hammer: tool for marking an ownership symbol on a pulp log

swamper: one who clears away trees and brush to build a camp or a road, and keeps logging roads in good shape

teamster: person who drives teams of horses

tend out: during a river drive, to stand watch along the shore of a river, particularly at points where log jams are likely to form, and to jump in when needed to keep logs moving

tote road: road to a logging camp along which supplies are hauled (toted)

tote team: horses and wagon, or sled, used to haul supplies into camp

turn out: short, wide area spaced along a two-sled road, where teams with empty sleds could turn out to allow loaded sleds to pass

twitch: to drag a log to the yard. Oxen and horses did the pulling. The trail was called a twitching road.

undercut: the notch cut into a tree with an ax, to fell it in the desired direction

walking boss: man in charge of two or more camps, sometimes called a superintendent. The name stems from early logging days, when he walked from camp to camp.

wangan [WAHN gan]: an American Indian word for camping place. It has many spellings (generally "wangan" in New England) and two distinct meanings to lumbermen: (1) camp store where lumbermen bought clothing and other articles. (2) wagons or bateaux on a river drive that moved supplies downriver.

watershed: drainage basin

yard: place to where horses twitched logs, to be later hauled by sleds to the landing

yardarm [YARD arm]: on a ship, a pole attached crosswise to a mast, to support additional sails

yarding crew: men who loaded logs onto sleds

TO LEARN MORE . . .

Additional Reading

Appelbaum, Diana K. *Giants in the Land.* Boston: Houghton Mifflin, 1993.

Cassie, Brian. *National Audubon Society First Field Guide: Trees.* New York: Scholastic, 1999.

Drake, Jane, with Ann Love. *Forestry.* Buffalo: Kids Can Press, 1996 and 1998.

Field, Eileen. *The Eastern Forest.* New York: Benchmark Books, 1997.

Grant, Alden. *Logging in the Maine Woods: The Paintings of Alden Grant.* Rangeley, Maine: Rangeley Lakes Region Logging Museum, 1994.

Kurelek, William. *Lumberjack.* Montreal: Tundra Books of Montreal, 1974.

Lasky, Kathryn. *Marven of the Great North Woods.* New York: Harcourt Brace, 1997.

Manning, Samuel F. *New England Masts and the King's Broad Arrow.* Gardiner, Maine: Tilbury House, 2000.

Shetterly, Susan Hand. *Shelterwood.* Gardiner, Maine: Tilbury House, 1999.

Videos

From Stump to Ship: A 1930 Logging Film. University of Maine at Orono and the Northeast Archives of Folklore and Oral History, 1985.

Woodsmen and River Drivers-—Another Day, Another Era. Northeast Archives of Folklore and Oral History, 1989.

Places to Visit

Adirondack Museum, Blue Mountain Lake, New York. Exhibit shows logging techniques similar to those used in New England. (518) 352-7311.
http://www.adkmuseum.org

Lumbermen's Museum, Patten, Maine. (207) 528-2650.
http://www.lumbermensmuseum.org

Maine Forest and Logging Museum, Leonard's Mills, Bradley, Maine. (207) 581-2871.
http://www.leonardsmills.com

Maine State Museum, Augusta, Maine. (207) 287-2301.
http://www.state.me.us/museum

Northern Forest Heritage Park, Berlin, New Hampshire. (603) 752-7202.
http://www.northernforestheritage.org

Web Sites

American Forests.
http://www.Americanforests.org

American Tree Farm System.
http://www.treefarmsystem.org

Appalachian Mountain Club.
http://www.outdoors.org

Certified Logging Program.
http://www.moosehead.net/clp

Game of Logging.
http://www. forestapps.com

Maine Forest Products Council.
http://www.maineforest.com

Maine Forest Service.
http://www.state.me.us/doc/mfs/

National Audubon Society.
http://www.audubon.org

Sierra Club.
http://www. sierraclub.org

Society of American Foresters.
http://www.safnet.org

USDA Forest Service.
http://www.fs.fed.us

Wilderness Society.
http://www.wilderness.org

SOURCE NOTES AND SELECTED BIBLIOGRAPHY

Hundreds of sources were used in writing this book, many more than are listed here. Main sources for overall information are followed by those used to prepare specific chapters:

Coolidge, Philip T. *History of the Maine Woods*. Bangor, ME: Furbush-Roberts Printing Company, Inc., 1963, 2nd printing 1966.

Cox, Thomas, Robert Maxwell, Phillip Thomas, and Joseph Malone. *This Well-Wooded Land*. Lincoln: University of Nebraska Press, 1985.

Dobbs, David, and Richard Ober. *The Northern Forest*. White River Junction, VT: Chelsea Green Publishing, 1995.

Holbrook, Stewart H. *Yankee Loggers*. New York: International Paper Company, 1961.

Judd, Richard W. *Aroostook: A Century of Logging in Northern Maine*. Orono: University of Maine Press, 1989.

Judd, Richard W., Edwin A. Churchill, and Joel W. Eastman, eds. *Maine. The Pine Tree State From Prehistory to the Present*. Orono: University of Maine Press, 1995.

Marchand, Peter J. *North Woods. An Inside Look at the Nature of Forests in the Northeast*. Boston: Appalachian Mountain Club, 1987.

Pike, Robert E. *Tall Trees, Tough Men*. New York: W. W. Norton & Company, 1967.

Smith, David C. *A History of Lumbering in Maine, 1861–1960*. Orono: University of Maine Press, 1972.

Wilkins, Austin H. *Ten Million Acres of Timber*. Woolwich, ME: TBW Books, 1978.

Wood, Richard G. *A History of Lumbering in Maine, 1820–1861*. Orono: University of Maine Press, 1961.

Chapters 1–2 (early history)

Carroll, Charles F. *The Timber Economy of Puritan New England.* Providence, RI: Brown University Press, 1973.

Manning, Samuel F. *New England Masts and the King's Broad Arrow*. Kennebunk, ME: Thomas Murphy, Publishers, 1979. Reissued by Tilbury House, Gardiner, ME: 2000.

Chapters 3-5 (logging and river driving)

Arndt, Christopher, Ph.D. *The Solid Men of Bangor: Economic, Business and Political Growth of Maine's Urban Frontier, 1769–1845*. Ann Arbor: University of Michigan, 1987.

Chaney, Michael P. *White Pine on the Saco River: An Oral History of River Driving in Southern Maine*. Northeast Folklore, vol. XXIX. Orono, ME: Maine Folklife Center, 1993.

Franco-American Studies Class, Hyde School, Bath, Maine. *Immigrants From the North*. Lewiston, ME: Pen Mor Printers, 1982.

McBride, Stewart D. "America's Last Log Drive." *Christian Science Monitor*, October 29, 1976, pp. 16–17.

Chapters 6–8 (sawmills, mechanization, and forest fires)

Hilton, David. *From York to the Allagash: Forest Fire Lookouts of Maine*. Greenville, ME: Moosehead Communications, 1997.

MacDougall, Walter M. "Lombard's Iron Monster." *Yankees Under Steam*. Austin N. Stevens, ed. Dublin, NH: Yankee, 1970, pp. 50–55.

Rivard, Paul E. *Maine Sawmills: A History*. Augusta: Maine State Museum, 1990.

Woodbury, George. *John Goffe's Mill*. New York: W. W. Norton, 1948.

Chapters 9-10 (current forestry and future predictions)

Frome, Michael. *The Forest Service*. Second Edition, revised and updated. Boulder, CO: Westview Press, 1984.

Irland, Lloyd C. *The Northeast's Changing Forest*. Petersham, MA: Harvard University Press, 1999.

Shepherd, Jack. *The Forest Killers. The Destruction of the American Wilderness*. New York: Weybright and Talley, 1975.

Wilkins, Austin H. *The Forests of Maine: Their Extent, Character, Ownership, and Products*. Augusta: Maine Forest Service, Bulletin No. 8, 1932.

Several personal accounts helped in creating the vignettes. Some of them are:

"A Tenderfoot At Hamlin's: Adventures of a 'City Feller' in a Maine Logging Camp." *Lewiston (Maine) Journal*, Illustrated Magazine Section. Three-Part Feature (January 1906).

Averill, Gerald. *Ridge Runner. The Story of a Maine Woodsman*. Philadelphia: J.B. Lippincott, 1948.

Ballew, Stephen, Joan Brooks, Dona Brotz, and Edward Ives. *"Suthin" (It's the Opposite of Nothin')*. Orono: University of Maine, Northeast Folklore, vol. XVIII, 1977.

Bartlett, Stanley F. *Beyond the Sowdyhunk*. Portland, ME: Falmouth Bookhouse, 1937.

Eckstorm, Fannie Hardy. *The Penobscot Man*. Somersworth: New Hampshire Publishing Co., 1972. (Facsimile of 1924 edition; new introduction by Edward Ives)

Farrington, Ervin S. *A Lumberjack at Thirteen*. Center Conway, NH: Walker's Pond Press and Advertising Company, 1982.

McKenny, C. Ross. *Language of the Forest*. Portsmouth, NH: Peter Randall Publishers, 1991.

Additional information came from magazine and newspaper articles, videos, and government publications. Research was conducted in several historical societies and museums. Helpful details came from the author's family archives relating to a logging operation in Crystal, New Hampshire; and from observations made on visits to sawmills, a fire tower, logging sites, state forests, and the White Mountain National Forest. Interviews and correspondence with forest rangers, loggers, and a number of corporate, independent, government, and educational foresters rounded out the research.

ACKNOWLEDGMENTS

For their help with research for this book, I would like to thank the following: Adirondack Museum; Sidney Balch; Bangor Public Library; Bates College Library; Berlin, New Hampshire and Coos County Historical Society; Bethel, Maine, Historical Society; Andrea Corbett; Department of Conservation/Maine Forest Service; James Downie; Barbara Frost; Hancock Lumber Company, Casco, Maine; Gregg Hesslein; International Paper Company; Edward "Sandy" Ives; Richard W. Judd; Jason L'Heureux; Lumbermen's Museum, Patten, Maine; Maine Forest and Logging Museum, Leonard's Mills; Maine Historic Preservation Commission; Maine Historical Society; Maine State Museum; Samuel Manning; Mark Mayhew; Stanley Marshall; MeadWestvaco/Forestry Division–New England Region; James Meehan; Patrick Moore; Northeast Archives of Folklore and Oral History, Maine Folklife Center, University of Maine; Northern Forest Heritage Park, Berlin, New Hampshire; Osher Map Library, Portland, Maine; Ossipee, Maine, Fire Tower; Peavey Manufacturing Co., Eddington, Maine; Rangeley Lakes Region Historical Society; Rangeley Lakes Region Logging Museum; Rodney Richard; Judith Round; Steven Sader; John Sinclair; Albert Soule; Tate House, Portland, Maine; University of Maine, College of Natural Sciences, Forestry, and Agriculture; Jack Wadsworth; White Mountain National Forest; G. Bruce Wiersma; Margaret R. Yocom; Jerry Young.

A word of appreciation goes to Jean Reynolds at Millbrook Press for her help in editing this book.

Special thanks to all my family for their constant support throughout the writing of this book: to my special "readers"—my mother, Erma Morton, sister, Margaret Stires, and son and daughter-in-law, Timothy and Marianne Cowan; my aunt, Helen Morton, who wrote down hundreds of details about living in our family's logging operation as a child; my husband, Carl, for his understanding and support of my desire to write this book, and for doing all kinds of chores so I could work, even fixing my computer occasionally; and to my father, Hugh Morton, who did not live long enough to see the book to completion, but who helped immensely, and who was the inspiration behind this whole project.

This book was made possible, in part, by an Anna Cross Giblin Nonfiction Grant from the Society of Children's Book Writers and Illustrators.

INDEX

Page numbers in *italics* refer to illustrations.

PICTURE CREDITS

Cover photograph courtesy of the Rangeley Lakes Region Logging Museum of Rangeley, Maine ("Cutting and Twitching Off a Hillside" by Alden Grant. 18 x 24 inches, oil on canvasboard, c. 1988.)

ABOUT THE AUTHOR

Mary Morton Cowan has always loved the woods, learning much about woods lore from her father, who grew up in a logging camp in New Hampshire. This book was inspired by many of his stories. Research revealed a more realistic picture of the difficulties and dangers of logging and its importance to New England culture. It also sparked an intense desire to share that knowledge with young readers. A special motivation to complete this book came when she received an Anna Cross Giblin Nonfiction Grant from the Society of Children's Book Writers and Illustrators.

A Maine native, Ms. Cowan grew up near an old mast landing, graduated from Bates College, and moved to Rochester, New York, for several years. She has written one historical novel, *Ice Country*, and more than fifty nonfiction articles and activities for children's magazines. This is her first nonfiction book. She and her husband now live on the edge of the woods in Maine.